The Art and Science of Investing in Gold

Dedicated to every investor who is willing to go against the herd

(in proper proportions, of course)

Also by James Park

Dividend Investing: A Guide to Building Sustainable Passive Income

Preparing For Financial Success

Beating The Market

The Self Made Investor
www.theselfmadeinvestor.com
theselfmadeinvestor@gmail.com

ISBN-978-1-7339722-6-0

Disclaimer: As investors, we assume risk in order to obtain a return. This book is geared towards investors looking to increase risk in an effort to achieve larger returns. As investors, we cannot guarantee the future of any market or the performance of any security. We invest at our own risk. We can take measures aimed at achieving the highest possible return for a given level of risk, but the risk of loss will always exist.

Follow us on Twitter:
https://twitter.com/MadeInvestor

About the Author

James Park is a CPA who spends his free time writing books about investing and personal finance. He believes in a self-directed, low-fee approach that relies on asset allocation and periodic rebalancing while applying more aggressive techniques in conservative increments. He has a BS in accounting from Franklin University and an MBA with a focus on finance from The Ohio State University.

"Dividend Investing" and "Preparing For Financial Success" both focus on building wealth through investments over the course of one's working years. "Beating The Market" focuses on ways to achieve higher returns by increasing risk in proper proportions. “The Art and Science of Investing in Gold” serves two distinct purposes: it teaches the retirement-minded investor how to hedge while also teaching the risk-averse investor how to pursue high returns at specific points in the economic cycle.

Table of Contents

Key Terms

The art of investing in gold: The practice of reading economic indicators in order to time entry and exit points in the gold market, thus enabling the investor to earn large returns in a short amount of time when opportunities arise.

The science of investing in gold: The practice of allocating at most 10% of a well-diversified portfolio to gold, and then rebalancing the portfolio periodically in order to exploit volatility in gold, thus enabling the investor to increase the size of their portfolio systematically over extended periods of time.

Modern Portfolio Theory: A framework for how risk-averse investors can construct their portfolio to get the highest possible return for a given level of risk. Investment funds are spread across a variety of asset classes with varying levels of correlation. Over time the allocation of the portfolio will change as some asset classes advance and others retreat. The investor will then sell a portion of the advancing securities and buy more of the retreating securities in order to get the portfolio back in balance. The science of investing in gold is that no more than 10% of the portfolio should be allocated to gold.

Side Bet: An investment one makes with disposable income that is in addition to their retirement savings. When one practices the art of investing in gold, it's wise to do so as a side bet, while the science of investing in gold is done simultaneously as part of a larger portfolio.

Fiat Currency: Government issued money that isn't backed by a commodity, like gold. The U.S. dollar became a fiat currency in 1971 when President Nixon took the currency off the gold standard.

Federal Reserve: The central banking system of the United States of America. They can increase the money supply by printing money and buying debt, either from the Treasury or on the open market.

Intrinsic Value: What an asset is worth, as opposed to what the asset is selling for. Intrinsic value is calculated by making projections of future earnings, discounting them back to present value, and summing the total. If the intrinsic value is higher than the current price, the asset is considered a candidate for investment.

Spot Price: The current price at which a given asset can be bought or sold for immediate delivery. When we refer to the price of gold, we refer to its spot price.

Strike Price: The price that a security can be bought or sold for according to the terms of an options contract. When a gold investor enters into a contract that provides the option to buy gold over the course of six months at a predetermined price, they lock in a strike price. The strike price that gold is exchanged for in the future will likely differ from the spot price on that date.

Introduction

If you've read any of my previous books, you know I like to start off by explaining what the book can't do for you. It's not because I'm a pessimist or have a lack of confidence in my work; rather, it's because I see value in creating realistic expectations. The investment world is an easy place to make money, but only if you understand *why* it's easy. If you have realistic expectations for the return that an investment can provide, as well as a firm understanding of the risk involved, then you're most of the way there. My job is to get you all of the way there.

I'd sell more books if I wasn't hung up on being realistic; *I'm certain of it.* The easiest way to boost book sales is to put the word "millionaire" in the title. It's an engaging word that conjures images of massive success and a life of leisure. If my goal was to sell as many books as possible—and let's face it, that's an incredibly realistic goal for a writer—the book in your hands would have been titled *The Art of Becoming A Millionaire With Gold.* By doing so I'd sell more books and you'd become detrimentally overconfident. It almost sounds like stealing, *doesn't it?*

Gold is a tricky market and your success in this market isn't guaranteed just because you read a book (be it my book or any book on investing in gold). Whether or not you become a millionaire is entirely up to you. Frankly, I think you can do it. I have confidence in you. But it's important to understand that an investment in gold alone isn't going to get you there. The puzzle of wealth has many pieces. Gold is just one of them. There are times when gold is the piece that holds the entire puzzle together. Other times you'll find yourself struggling over a piece that doesn't seem to fit anywhere.

If you want to succeed as an investor, then the amount that you save and contribute to your investments is the most important piece. Gold has a tendency to outperform the stock market by leaps and bounds during specific intervals in the economic cycle. When this happens, it's an opportunity to increase the size of your portfolio while the rest of the world is biting their fists and waiting for stocks to recover. The ability to identify trends in gold is important, but it's only useful if you have capital to invest. You can't compensate for a poor savings regimen by chasing unrealistically high returns. Gold provides the return that it provides when it provides it. There's no arguing with that. At the same time, it's really hard to save your way to millionaire. You need investments, too.

The stock market tends to experience longer bull runs than gold. During periods of economic expansion, stocks can go higher than they rightfully should. This is where most investors place their attention. People who don't invest but watch the news still have a vague sense of what the stock market is doing. As long as people keep buying stocks, the market will continue to set new highs. When enough people get behind it, the stock market can spend more than a decade trending higher. This rarely happens with gold. When gold gets its turn at bat, it has the propensity to deliver large gains in a short amount of time. Wealth is transferred during these short bursts. Investors who've mastered the art of investing in gold can make a lot of money when there's a runup in gold. But when the runup is over, those still holding the bag will face devastating losses.

Gold provides an opportunity to earn large returns during specific stages of the economic cycle, but we don't have to be market timers to recognize the benefits of this precious metal. When held in a fully diversified portfolio, a modest allocation to gold can be used to increase long-term returns while simultaneously reducing risk exposure. That's the science of investing in gold. It will get you closer to becoming a millionaire, not because you went all-in on gold, but because you saved, you diversified your portfolio, and you used gold to improve your position. The science of investing in gold is very systematic. You're going to learn that anyone can do it. The art of investing in gold, on the other hand, is challenging. Large gains over short spans of time don't come easily. It requires skill, it entails risk, and it opens the door for one to make errors and succumb to poor judgment. Throughout the book I'll make the argument that everyone should practice the science of investing in gold. I'm a proponent of modern portfolio theory and I strongly believe that gold deserves a place in most portfolios. But when it comes to the art of investing in gold, discretion is advised. The artist isn't content with market returns. Instead of allowing their investments to work through cycles and return large gains in due time, they go in search of bull markets that will bring them gains now. They view investing as an intellectual pursuit. There's nothing wrong with that, as long as one has the proper temperament and is willing to accept that markets will at times move against them. We can all be scientists, but we can't all be artists. You might already know whether market timing is for you. If it's early in your progression as an investor, you might still be cultivating your approach. Whatever the case, I encourage all readers to engage with the material on the art of investing in gold. It might inspire you to dip your toes in the water and then become an artist. If nothing more, it will enable you to better appreciate why the science of investing in gold is so reliable.

The market timing strategies we'll discuss aren't intended for your retirement savings. Everyone needs a secure retirement. A long-term buy-and-hold strategy is an easy and effective way to get there. The artist shouldn't forgo the basic principles of financial planning. They should save for retirement first and then use discretionary income to practice their art. I like to think of it as making a side bet. When you're confident that gold is going to move higher, then it's time to trim some fat from your budget in order to chase those high returns with money that you'd have otherwise spent. Or, given that your retirement is already on track, you allocate a modest amount of money toward market timing endeavors each month. Gold, when held outside of a diversified portfolio, can be risky, but there are ways to control for risk while chasing large returns. Making the investment with money you can afford to lose is an effective control. It's also easier to maintain a strong psychology when your standard of living isn't tied to the direction that gold moves over the next few months. That's what side bets are for. It sounds like gambling, but it's more strategic than that. We're not trying to predict the next spin of the roulette wheel; we're simply implementing a strategy as we control for the probability of the market moving against us.

The strategies we'll focus on aren't difficult, but it requires some intestinal fortitude to put money at risk in an effort to build wealth. A bull run in gold doesn't come from nowhere. The economic indicators are very identifiable. The stock market is overheated, interest rates keep getting cut, central banks are stocking up on gold, there have been rounds of quantitative easing, and everyone is, or at least should be, worried that inflation is coming. This is the type of environment where it pays to be long on gold. It's up to you to read the economic indicators and implement a strategy that not only aligns with your skillset, but also with your tolerance for risk. The signals are easy to read, but they can't be rushed. The art of investing in gold requires patience. If the signals aren't flashing, then they're not flashing. The fact that you didn't pick a book with the word "millionaire" in the title is a good sign. You're not looking for a quick solution, but instead want to understand gold investing for what it is.

Every investor has their own style. When it comes to gold there are three predominant approaches: (1) invest in gold at the right stage in the economic cycle, (2) hold modest amounts of gold as a hedge in a well-diversified portfolio, and (3) buy it and bury it in your back yard. We're going to discuss all three. The first approach is the art, the second approach is the science, and the third approach is more or less insurance against the risk of our currency losing value.

The buy it and bury it in your back yard approach will receive the least amount of attention. It's an approach often utilized by prophets of doom and gloom who don't believe that a fiat currency is worth . . . *well, they don't believe that it's worth its weight in gold.* They question the logic of holding money that isn't backed by anything except for the good faith of the issuing government. A dollar bill only holds value if the population continues to subscribe to the theory that it holds value. When the theory becomes impaired, the purchasing power of gold remains intact as the purchasing power of the currency disintegrates. This is why some investors prefer a buy-and-hold strategy. They don't care about the ups and downs. Instead, they care about having enough gold when their fiat currency fails. It's not as much about making money as it is about protecting what they've already built. If the financial system collapses, all of the assets held in online brokerage accounts could become worthless. A physical asset like gold still holds value. The same can be said for real estate. Physical assets provide a sense of security that you can't get from stocks and bonds. Some of the strategies we'll use to build wealth rely on index funds that are stored and traded exactly like a share of stock. In doing so, we forgo the security of a physical asset in favor of the convenience of a fund that can be traded on an exchange. In most cases, we prefer the convenience because it enables us to more conveniently time the market. But once the wealth has been built, gold as a form of insurance becomes more appealing. Don't worry, it doesn't necessarily have to be buried in your back yard. In Chapter 4, we're going to discuss all the different ways to buy and store gold.

While gold can be used to accumulate wealth at specific stages in the economic cycle, over extended periods of time it simply maintains its value. Gold is a commodity, just like oil, wheat, corn, cattle, Patagonian aardvarks, cannabis, potatoes, plutonium, and other precious metals like silver. Coffee is also a commodity. In fact, it's an incredibly popular commodity. More than 450 million cups of coffee are consumed in the United States every day. Some of us can't start our day, let alone make it all the way through the day, without coffee. I love coffee. It wakes me up and helps me focus on my investments. As long as I avoid the cheapest varieties on the market, I can also say that it tastes really good. I know in advance that the price I pay for coffee is going to change. In the short run, it will fluctuate. Today I paid $1.50 for a cup of coffee; tomorrow I might pay $1.65, or maybe $1.45. Down the road I might end up paying $6.95, but I'm hoping to be an old man before that happens. I can't say for sure what a cup of coffee will cost in five years, but it's almost certain to be more than it costs today. The important distinction here is that it's the *price* that keeps changing. The value that a cup of coffee provides is constant. I enjoy drinking it today and I anticipate that I will extract the same enjoyment from drinking it in five years. Nothing about the coffee is expected to change. My desire to consume coffee won't change, but the amount of money I have to part with in order to drink coffee is definitely going to change. In other words, coffee is expected to stay the same while the purchasing power of money is expected to decline.

If I want to take money today and set it aside to buy coffee five years from today, I need to invest in an asset class that at a minimum won't decline in value, and might even increase in value. I could buy stocks, bonds, real estate, or gold. Some people invest in fine art. Some prefer wine. Others speculate on cryptocurrencies. We're going to discuss the unique intricacies of different asset classes with an emphasis on how they compare to gold. For now, keep in mind that gold is a commodity. Like coffee, it maintains its value. Unlike coffee, it's not necessarily bought and sold for personal consumption. Gold is used to make jewelry and other valuable items, but what really drives the price of gold is the action of investors. When central banks buy and sell gold in large quantities, the price adjusts accordingly. When you or I buy and sell gold, we do so at a price that's already set. But if enough individual investors move in unison, we too can influence the price. The demand for gold is different than the demand for coffee. The typical coffee drinker consumes coffee on a daily basis, through both good times and bad. The demand for coffee is relatively constant. Gold is different. When the economic forecast turns dreary, the demand for gold increases.

The impact of inflation is that it takes more dollars to buy gold. If you bought gold before inflation set in, you can now sell your gold for more dollars. By investing in gold, we protect the purchasing power of our savings. It's easy to do, yet most people don't bother. Precious metals comprise less than one-half of 1% of all savings in the U.S., which means that most of these savings will decline in value. When gold is held over the long-term as an insurance policy, it doesn't make us rich, but it provides protection nonetheless. If we take it a step further and increase our exposure to gold as the economic outlook darkens, and then decrease our exposure when rays of sunshine start poking through the clouds, we increase our propensity to build wealth. They say that wealth isn't destroyed during a stock market crash; instead, wealth is transferred, and those who hold gold are on the receiving end of the transfer. We're going to discuss strategies that enable us to increase our exposure to gold both before and during a stock market crash. Similarly, we're going to discuss strategies that enable us to increase our exposure to gold when the prospect of inflation is high.

Some of the strategies we'll discuss combine the art and science of investing in gold. Economic indicators lend themselves to the art, while the act of rebalancing your portfolio lends itself to the science. Financial markets aren't static, but constantly evolving. Patterns can disintegrate just as quickly as they form. When gold is used as a hedge, we're not so much concerned with the entry and exit points, but with how gold behaves relative to the other holdings. The buy low, sell high mechanism happens naturally through the act of rebalancing. If you've read either of my first two releases, *Dividend Investing* and *Preparing For Financial Success*, you're well-versed in the benefits of rebalancing. If not, don't worry. You're going to get more than just a crash course. And it won't be a redundant read if you already grasp the concept. We're going to take a gold-centric look at modern portfolio theory and the benefits of rebalancing. Gold is a unique asset class. There's no random walk or efficient market hypothesis. It's not a business that can be mismanaged, nor is it a business that might develop a revolutionary new product. It doesn't pay a dividend, there aren't any stakeholders to keep happy, and it's never going to file Chapter 11 bankruptcy. The poor performance that some publicly traded companies exhibit isn't applicable to gold. The stellar performance that other publicly traded companies exhibit isn't the driving factor. That's why gold is such a powerful tool. It's not correlated to the stock market, it's not correlated to the real estate market, and during periods of economic contraction when everyone's thankful that they allocated at least some of their portfolio to bonds, gold has the propensity to do even better. We can use it to hedge through all stages of the economic cycle. Then, when the time is right, we can make a side bet in gold.

When the early signs of a bull run in gold are present, we'll use discretionary income to time the market. Now we're building wealth even faster. The most important caveat is that we can't rush the market timing aspect of our strategy. We only want to make a side bet in gold when the time is right. During periods of economic expansion stocks are going to perform better, bonds are going to pay interest, and the price of gold tends to decline. The power of a side bet is that it provides an opportunity to get funds in the right asset class at the right time. The drawback, of course, is that markets don't always behave as expected. We never want to implement a strategy that requires us to time the turning point, but if we can time the bull run with even a modest amount of accuracy, large gains can be had. It's an achievable goal, but you have to be patient. Gold isn't always on the up-and-up. The bear markets can be devastating.

In college, I had a finance professor who taught the class that when you buy gold, you actually want it to decline in price. You read that right. When you use gold to hedge your portfolio, you actually want the price to go down. When it does, it means your other investments are probably doing just fine. When stocks are in rally mode, there's a reasonable chance that gold is doing just the opposite. You won't see the true benefit of your gold allocation until stocks stop doing their job. It makes sense that gold, as a hedge, should comprise a small part of the portfolio. When measured against the number of dollars currently in circulation, there's a limit to how high gold can go. The stock market, on the other hand, has no such limit. Every company is different, but their overarching objectives can all be summed up in a single statement; they exist to create value. They aren't all successful at it, but the stock market as a whole is a measure of the value that's created. The propensity to create value cannot be capped. It's limited only by the ability of those who work for publicly traded companies. Some companies fail, others scrape by, and some continue to create more and more value. The same cannot be said about gold. There's a fixed amount of gold on planet Earth. While we continue to drill for gold and therefore increase the amount in circulation, the amount that exists on our planet is still fixed. There's only so much gold above the ground and there's only so much gold beneath the ground. *That's it!* The price of gold cannot increase indefinitely. In order for the price to rise, the value of the currency that we measure gold against must decline. A currency can only decline as far as zero, which means that gold cannot rise indefinitely. There are times when gold accelerates, but gold cannot create infinite value. Like the stock market, it eventually reaches a ceiling and declines. Unlike the stock market, we should not assume that the subsequent recovery will lead to a new record high.

When stocks are down, there's an 83% chance that gold is up. But when stocks are up, gold could be doing just about anything. The fully diversified investor doesn't complain when all of their assets are in an upswing. She also understands that this isn't practical, at least not for extended periods of time. She's content when gold loses value because she understands that it will eventually come through and pack a punch when nothing else is getting the job done.

I'm a firm believer that wealth is infinite. The 1% are not in the 1% because they take from the remaining 99%, but because they either create value or they own assets that create value. Some do both. Everyone has an opportunity to build wealth by doing work that creates value and then investing the proceeds in the stock of companies that also create value. Even as companies compete, the stakeholders can diversify their interests across many companies so that no one truly loses. When dividends are paid, we rejoice collectively. As long as our species continues to do innovative work, we all have the ability to improve our financial wellbeing. The art of investing in gold provides an opportunity to improve it even faster, but it's not a collective endeavor. Instead of buying into a market that's going to expand over time, we buy into a market that's finite. A bull market in gold is not the result of a society collectively sharing in the fruits of its labor. It means those who bought gold at the right time are doing better than those who sold gold at the wrong time. The artist is always asking, *is now the time to buy gold?* That's the magic question. We'll devote Chapters 6, 7, and 8 to answering this question.

From there, we'll discuss gold mining stocks and cryptocurrencies as alternative methods of investing in gold. Gold mining stocks can be used as a leveraged investment for the risk-tolerant investor who wants to chase even bigger returns. Cryptocurrencies, while different from gold, exhibit many similarities. Investors treat them like digital gold. In Chapter 10, we'll discuss strategies for investing in this highly volatile market. The Millennials are embracing the world of cryptocurrencies. They understand the advantages of a currency that, like gold, isn't maintained by a government. The nagging question is, which cryptocurrency(s) are going to earn consumer acceptance.

In Chapter 11, we'll discuss the disadvantages of investing in gold. In the first paragraph of this introduction I stated that I'm not a pessimist. I intend to stand by that statement, but it doesn't mean I can't be a realist. Gold is not the be-all-end-all of investments. It's a hedge against many things, including trouble with inflation, fiat currencies, and stocks. It's also an excellent market timing tool during specific stages of the economic cycle. It is not, however, an asset class you can invest in whenever it strikes your fancy. The scientist outperforms over the long-term as a result of patience and reliance on a variety of asset classes. The artist outperforms in the short-term as a result of skill. The insurer already has wealth and wants to prepare for a worst-case scenario. The investor who chases gold without first taking time to learn about gold has a lot to lose. My goal is to provide the knowledge you need to make informed decisions in a market that's characterized by volatility.

In Chapter 12, we'll focus on alternative investments you might turn to in the future. The strategies we use to build wealth should differ from the strategies we use to maintain wealth. As a hedge, gold is a valuable holding no matter where you are in life. As a market timing tool, gold can be used to build wealth, but it should not be used to maintain wealth. Asset classes like stocks and real estate are better suited for this endeavor. We're going to be aggressive with gold when the time is right, but there's no sense in pushing the envelope once the job is done.

Then, in Chapter 13, we'll conclude with everyone's favorite topic—*taxes!* I won't spoil the surprise with an overly detailed preview here in the introduction. Instead, I promise to make the chapter as informative and painless as possible.

The gold investor has a rare opportunity to gain knowledge that many will never acquire. Gold is the oldest form of money that we have, but universities stopped teaching about gold in economics classes after most globally recognized currencies were taken off the gold standard. The result is that the younger generations don't understand the economics of gold. This, in part, explains why gold only accounts for less than one-half of 1% of all savings in the U.S. If you understand how gold functions as a currency, you either attended college before 1971 or you're self-taught. But how valuable is this knowledge? For those who successfully master the art of investing in gold, it's incredibly valuable. For those who stick solely to the science, value rests in the fact that their march towards financial independence will be one of reduced risk and noticeably higher rewards. That's the advantage of gold.

Chapter 1: How Rare Is Gold?

Let's pour ourselves a cup of coffee and return to our example from the introduction. Demand drives the price of gold. It's different than the demand for coffee because the demand for gold doesn't persist in a constant state. The number of people who start their morning with a cup of coffee isn't going to change dramatically over the next ten years (unless we find scientific evidence that coffee provides superhuman powers . . . causes a rapid increase in brain cells . . . prevents cancer . . . or who knows. . .). Barring that which is both unknown and unlikely, we don't expect dramatic changes in coffee consumption. There's both a steady demand and a steady supply, so we anticipate that coffee will remain affordable and the price will increase in line with the average rate of inflation. We can't say the same about gold. Demand fluctuates against a relatively fixed supply. There's a limited amount of gold on this planet. There's only so much in circulation above the earth's surface and only so much waiting to be found beneath the earth's surface.

Some argue that the supply of gold isn't truly "fixed" because we don't know for certain how much gold exists beneath the earth. Excavation is an important step in the gold mining process. Some excavations are extremely successful, while others are completely fruitless. Even after gold has been found, the question of how deep to drill comes into play. The deeper the gold is buried, the more expensive the extraction. According to the World Gold Council, a total of 190,000 tons of gold have already been extracted from the earth. On average, between 2,500 and 3,000 tons of gold are mined annually, thereby increasing the amount of gold in circulation by approximately 1.4% each year. Unless we find ways to increase the rate at which gold is mined, the amount of gold extracted as a percent of gold in circulation will gradually decline. This further solidifies that notion that the gold supply is relatively fixed, while the demand can fluctuate significantly.

Unlike the price of coffee, the price of gold doesn't increase in line with inflation. In fact, when inflation proceeds at a healthy rate, say somewhere in the neighborhood of 3% annually, the price of gold could easily move in the opposite direction. This surprises most people, but it's true. Even though gold serves as a reliable hedge against high inflation, its behavior is less predictable during periods of low to moderate inflation. If you're looking for a short-term store of value, gold is a risky bet. We anticipate that gold will catch up with inflation in due time, but it's difficult to predict in advance how many years this will take. Basically, we're waiting for inflation to become so much of a problem that everyone turns their attention to gold, which causes a revaluation to occur. When this happens, the price of gold advances leaps and bounds over a short span of time. It not only makes up for all those years when the price of gold failed to keep pace with healthy levels of inflation, but also compensates for the current period of high inflation. That's why bull runs in gold tend to be short and fierce. A lot of money can be made during these bursts. When inflation returns to a healthy state, gold will fall, and the bear market that follows has the potential to be nasty.

But how rare is gold? If we're going to master the art of investing in gold, we need to know how much of it actually exists on earth. In addition to the 190,000 tons currently in circulation, the World Gold Council estimates that 54,000 tons of gold exists below the earth in sufficient concentrations that are accessible to be mined at reasonable cost. This means that according to current estimates, the amount of gold in circulation could increase by 28% over the next 20 years, and that's it. There's always the possibility that there's more gold to be found. Or, extraction methods could be improved, therefore allowing greater quantities of gold to be mined at reasonable cost. We also know that at least some gold exists on other planets, but we don't yet know how much is out there. The prevailing belief is that gold was formed on Earth approximately 3.9 billion years ago as a result of a meteor crash. Conceivably, this could happen again, either on our planet or elsewhere. But making investment decisions based on the probability of this happening again is futile. You'd be better off speculating on penny stocks. At the time of writing, the gold market factors in a fixed quantity of 244,000 tons on planet Earth. Until significantly larger reserves are discovered, gold will continue to function as a precious metal where demand fluctuates against a fixed supply.

Gold is indestructible. Even when melted down, it's not destroyed. It will remain in liquid form until it solidifies. So it's believed that all of the gold that's been mined still exists. At one point the United States had possession of 2/3 of the gold in circulation, but the demographics have changed. China and India are huge consumers of gold, not just as investments, but to make jewelry and other objects. They account for approximately 40% of current gold consumption. Today, the amount of gold in circulation is believed to be evenly distributed throughout the world. It's also estimated that millions of dollars worth of gold has found its way to the bottom of the ocean. It makes you wonder how many pirates lost their lives as this happened. If you're adventurous, you could go in search of it. If you're like me, you'll sit in a cubicle all day and simply invest in gold when the opportunity is ripe.

Compared to other commodities, the amount of gold in circulation is small. The coal reserves in America alone stand at 255 billion tons. More steel is created every hour than all of the gold that's been extracted in human history. Gold is also ten times rarer than silver. It's estimated that more than 1.6 million tons of silver have been mined throughout history and that 530,00 million tons remain beneath the earth. The largest silver reserves in the world belong to Peru, Australia, and Poland. Combined, they own almost 270,000 tons of silver, while there are only 190,000 tons of gold in circulation worldwide.

To put the scarcity of gold in a different perspective, if everyone in the world decided to invest in gold, at the current price there is enough in circulation for each of us to own about

$1,500 worth. Now, subtract the amount currently held by central banks, which accounts for about 20% of the gold in circulation, and the amount left for individual investors falls to 152,000 tons, or about $1,200 worth per person. Searching for gold on the ocean floor instead of sitting in a cubicle all day is starting to sound like a tempting proposition.

While gold is rare, it's important to note the gold derivatives are not. That's the void that derivatives are designed to fill. Such instruments allow you to wager on the movement of the price of an asset without actually buying the asset. There's only 190,000 tons of gold in circulation, but there's no limit to the number of futures and options contracts that can be issued. This enables the amount of gold invested in at any given time to exceed the amount of gold that actually exists. My advice is to avoid most derivatives, not just for gold, but for any investment. Derivatives do serve a beneficial purpose, but are too often used as an instrument for speculation. In Chapter 4, we'll discuss a couple non-speculative strategies to protect ourselves with derivatives. Derivatives also serve an important function to those involved in the mining and distribution of gold. Aside from these functions, overreliance on derivatives can be dangerous. Our goal here is to master the art and science of investing. We'll leave speculating to the gamblers.

Chapter 2: A Brief History

Gold has a long, complex, fascinating, and at times bloody history. Nations of modest origin have built themselves into superpowers by accumulating gold. Investors have built insurmountable wealth by holding gold at the most opportune times in the economic cycle. And wars have been won and lost all in the name of gold. Hitler, for example, wasn't just trying to accumulate all the real estate in the world; he also wanted gold. German forces seized gold not just from the personal holdings of Jewish citizens, but from many central banks throughout Europe. The largest physical transfer of wealth that the world has ever recorded took place as the United Kingdom transported billions of dollars' worth of gold bullion to Canada for safekeeping.

Had Hitler been successful, it's safe to assume that gold would not be measured globally in U.S. dollars, as it is today. Instead, the Euro would never have come into existence, the Reichsmark would be the recognized global currency, and gold would naturally be valued according to this currency.

The history of gold is as varied as the number of societies who've accepted gold as a form of money. After World War II, the United States initiated what is known as the Bretton Woods Agreement, an order intended to govern monetary relations among independent countries, including the United States, Canada, Western Europe, Australia, and Japan. Each participating country was required to tie their currency to gold, and therefore create a system where exchange rates would only fluctuate at most by 1%. If a larger imbalance arose, the International Monetary Fund would bridge the imbalance of payments. The agreement fixed the value of $35 USD to one troy ounce of gold. Other currencies were then calibrated with the U.S. dollar at fixed rates.

From 1933 through 1974, it was illegal for a U.S. citizen to own gold. Instead, they could own the U.S. dollar, which was backed by gold. Executive Order 6102 was put in place by President Roosevelt on April 5, 1933. By the time President Ford legalized private ownership of gold coins, bars, and certificates on December 31, 1974, global monetary policy had radically changed. The U.S. dollar (along with many other major currencies) was no longer backed by gold.

President Nixon terminated the Bretton Woods Agreement on August 15, 1971 when he took the U.S. off the gold standard. The U.S. was now operating under a fiat currency, a change that's often referred to as "the Nixon shock." Since then, systems of fiat currencies have been enacted across the globe, with exchange rates established between each pair of currencies. Switzerland was one of the last countries to abandon the gold standard, which they eventually did in 1999.

While it's true that the U.S. dollar has lost value since we abandoned the gold standard, it should be noted that prior to World War II the U.S. abandoned the gold standard on two separate occasions. Nixon didn't take us into unchartered territory, but instead took us into territory that is somewhat predictable. There's an obvious advantage to holding a currency that's finite in quantity, but no currency is completely free from manipulation, including those backed by gold and other precious metals. The act of adding zinc, nickel, or copper to gold and silver coins has the same impact as printing more paper money. It artificially increases the amount of currency in circulation, which depreciates the value of the currency.

While true gold buffs will tell you that taking the U.S. dollar off the gold standard had drastic repercussions, it should be noted that there are some distinct advantages to a fiat currency. For starters, it doesn't fix government spending to the amount of gold in circulation. When the U.S. government issued assistance during the coronavirus pandemic, they were able to do so because we're on a fiat currency. The ability to print money comes with both advantages and disadvantages. The ability to print modest amounts of currency enables us to progress beyond the confines of our gold reserve. It only turns ugly when too much currency is printed in a short period of time.

The gold standard presents administrative difficulties that don't exist with a fiat currency. Ensuring that all of the currency in circulation is tied physically to gold is no easy task. No system is without flaw. The amount of currency in circulation prior to Nixon relieving the U.S. of the gold standard did not tie to the amount of gold in reserve. In this regard, it can be argued that the U.S. dollar didn't truly adhere to the gold standard, and Nixon simply made it official. Additionally, the opportunity for gold investors to earn large returns increases under a fiat currency, *and that's what this book is about!*

The act of a country taking their currency off the gold standard comes with obvious consequences. The currency loses considerable value and it therefore takes more units of the currency to purchase gold. The price of gold when measured in U.S. dollars skyrocketed as a result of the Nixon shock. In a single day, gold moved from $42 to $120 per ounce. By the end of the decade it had reached $459. Some might argue that gold increased in value as a result of the U.S. abandoning the gold standard, but this simply isn't true. Gold is still gold, just like coffee is still coffee. The change had no impact on the amount of gold in circulation. Instead of gold becoming more valuable, the U.S. dollar had become less valuable. Those who began purchasing gold in 1975, after it became legal to do so in the U.S., protected themselves from further devaluation in the purchasing power of the U.S. dollar. That's what gold truly is. It's an insurance policy against the decline of fiat currency. As we move into Chapters 6 and 7, we'll see that there are periods in the economic cycle when holding these insurance policies is more lucrative than others. The risk of holding too many insurance policies through every stage of the economic cycle is that during most of the stages, larger returns are available on the stock market.

The world powers no longer back their currencies with gold, but they still demand and stockpile gold in large quantities. This solidifies the ideology that gold is the only true money we have and everything else is just a currency. Or, as JP Morgan said in 1912, "Gold is money, everything else is credit." When we hold a fiat currency, be it in the form of dollar bills stuffed under the mattress or savings held in a money market account, it means that the country which issued the currency is in debt to us. We can exchange this debt for goods and services, but it's debt nonetheless. Only when we use this debt to purchase gold or other assets do we truly acquire wealth. Most individuals don't hold any wealth, but instead hold currency. Most developed countries, on the other hand, hold significant amounts of wealth.

In 2018 central banks across the globe collectively purchased 651 tons of gold. It's important for the gold investor to understand the impact that central banks have on the price of gold. With most assets that trade on an exchange, like stocks, it's the buying and selling of institutional investors that determines the price. This includes buying and selling done by mutual funds, hedge funds, insurance companies, and pension plans. With gold, it's the demand of central banks that truly sets the price. It's not just the individual investor who gets scared and turns to gold as a safe haven. Even though the gold standard was abandoned long ago, governments still desire the safety of gold and they increase their holdings during times of uncertainty.

The impact that a single country can have on the price of gold by implementing a change to their monetary policy is impressive. On June 6, 2016, when Great Britain voted to leave the European Union, otherwise known as Brexit, gold jumped from $1,254.96 to $1,347.12 per ounce over the course of six hours. Naturally, an investor shouldn't attempt to time this type of rapid increase by buying gold the day before the vote and then getting out the next day. This type of strategy is better suited for gamblers than investors. What goes up 7.34% in a single day can easily drop 10% (or more) the following day. Instead of timing a single announcement that could heavily impact the price of gold, we want to time the environment. Voting to leave the European Union is an event that could have gone one of two ways (and had it gone the other way, we'd have seen a large one-day drop in the price of gold). A savvy gold investor will play the period of uncertainty leading up to such a change and then sit on the sideline the day the change takes place. The period of uncertainty is a given, the reaction to the change is not. Between the vote on June 6, 2016 and the eventual, and at times questionable, withdrawal on January 31, 2020, gold increased by 32% while the FTSE 100 declined by 6%.

We could go further back in history. Gold coins have been in circulation since at least 800 B.C. We could study gold in terms of eastern currencies rather than western currencies. There's no shortage of economic data. The layered history of this precious metal is fascinating. We're fortunate that gold has a long history to analyze in order to implement a strategy. Aside from land, it has a longer history than any other asset class. If a stock investor wants to analyze the performance of the S&P 500, they can only go back as far as 1926, when the index was first created. The bond investor has even fewer options. While bonds have been in existence since early 1590, the bond index is a newer phenomenon. They weren't steadily maintained until the 1970s, which means that the index fund investor has significantly less data at his disposal. The cryptocurrency investor faces even greater challenges. Bitcoin was released to the public in January 2009. The history is much too short for analysts to identify meaningful trends. Instead, we're learning about cryptocurrencies as the trends are formed. Gold, on the other hand, is the oldest form of money in the world. Not only do we have greater than 5,000 years' worth of data to analyze, but we can observe the behavior of gold in countless economic situations across the globe.

How much history do we need to understand in order to competently master the art of investing in gold? The sagest wisdom I know is that one should never enter into an investment unless they understand how the investment provides a return. In the following chapter we'll dive deeper into the application of this advice. For now, let's focus on gold in terms of modern history. We've had a brief overview of how monetary policies have influenced the price of gold. With this history in mind, let's take a closer look at changes in the price of gold between 1971, when the United States abandoned the gold standard, and 2020, when the coronavirus pandemic swept across the globe and investors turned to gold for safety.

1971 – 1980

On August 15, 1971 President Nixon ended the Bretton Woods Agreement and rendered the U.S. dollar a fiat currency. If we compare the performance of gold to that of the S&P 500 from 1971 through 1980, the results are shocking. It looks like the S&P 500 hardly budges, when in fact it increased by 47.33%. It started 1971 at 92.15 and closed 1980 at 135.76. This isn't a huge gain. Over the course of 10 years we should expect, on average, that an investment in the stock market will at least double. It doesn't happen here, but 47.33% is a lot better than nothing. The reason it looks like nothing is because the S&P 500 is sharing the chart with an asset that increased by nearly 1300%. Naturally, this chart makes a bullish argument for simply buying gold bullion and burying it in your back yard. The good times don't last forever. Gold took a 26-year nap after this period of overperformance, while the stock market took a turn running with the bulls.

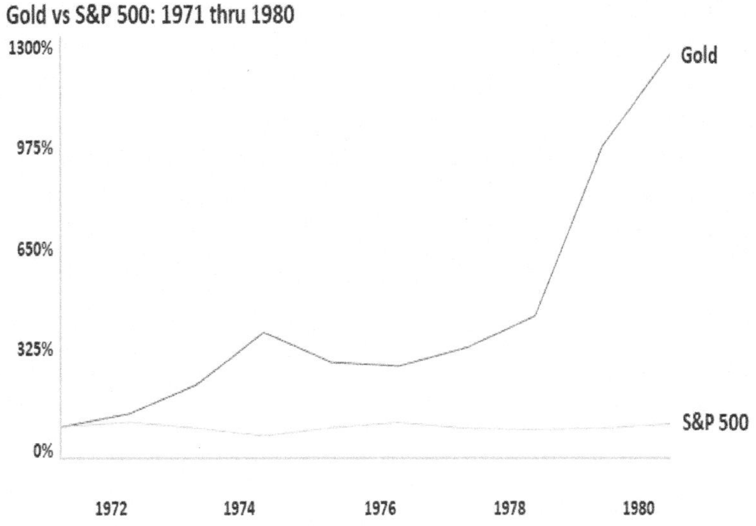

It should be noted that the initial bout between stocks and gold wasn't a fair fight. When Nixon took the U.S. off the gold standard, the price of gold rose from $42 to $120 in a single day. That's almost 300%. We shouldn't expect stocks to keep pace—*at first*. This, of course, is an anomaly and we shouldn't factor this type of reaction into a modern strategy. We were removed from the gold standard on August 15, 1971 and we're still off of the gold standard at the time of writing, which is almost fifty years later. In order for this event to recur, the gold standard would need to first be readopted. What we have experienced time and again since 1971 is the incessant printing of fiat currency, all while the gold supply remains constant. As we move into subsequent periods, we'll see that the printing of money has a bullish impact on gold, but when inflation isn't high, gold can go into slumber.

1980 – 2000

We've established that gold is not a buy-and-hold asset unless it's being used as a modest hedge. In order to build wealth exclusively from gold, it's an asset class that needs to be timed.

The 1970s was a bullish decade for gold. Investors who continued holding gold into the 1980s and even through the 1990s gave back a sizable portion of their gains. The investor who waited until the 1980s to jump on the bandwagon lost a lot of money. Again, it's difficult to observe price movements when an asset class that hardly budges shares a chart with an asset class that delivers huge returns. In this case, gold lost 32% over the course of 20 years, while the S&P 500 increased by 920%.

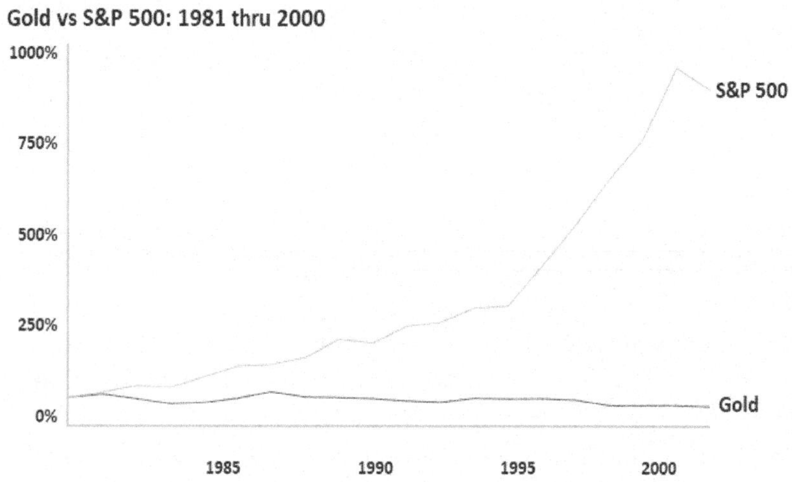

It should be noted that isolated bullish movement in gold did occur between 1981 and 2000. The savvy investor who either used gold as a hedge or managed to time these runs made money. The buy-and-hold investor, on the other hand, wouldn't be rewarded until the following decade.

2001 – 2011

From 2001 through 2011 gold reigned high and mighty, providing returns in excess of 450%. The S&P 500, on the other hand, took investors on a turbulent ride. It starts in recovery mode after the dot-com bubble burst. Then we have the 9/11 terrorist attacks in 2001, followed by the financial crisis of 2007-2008. The decade sees stocks rise and fall, rise and fall.

When I say that gold took a 26-year nap, which is a phenomenon that we'll keep returning to, what I mean is that gold peaked in 1980 at a little over $590 per ounce and didn't return to this level until 2006. The bear markets that follow a runup in gold can be brutal. By 2000, gold had been beaten down to the $270 range. Investors who got in at this level would see their investments more than double by the time a new high was set in 2006. The investor who bought in 1980, on the other hand, would have to wait 26 years before their investment showed a positive return. During this time, they could have built their retirement in the stock market. Gold can leave an investor empty handed for prolonged periods of time. Stocks have a history of always bouncing back and then going on to set new highs. Even when stocks enter into a "lost decade," the stock investor is still rewarded for seeing things through.

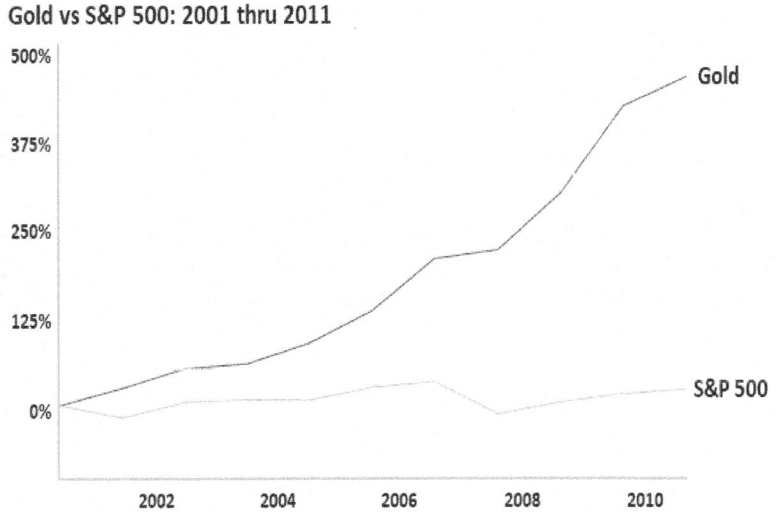

Contrary to what the chart indicates, the stock investor who maintained a buy-and-hold position between 2001 through 2011 actually improved their position. It all comes down to the fact that stocks pay dividends. When markets are flat, or at least manage to end where they started after a period of volatility, the investor who reinvests their dividends along the way progressively improves their position. They increase the number of shares that they own, which in turn not only leads to larger capital gains as stocks recover, but also increases their dividend income. There's a compounding effect at play that the gold investor doesn't receive. Gold lost 32% between 1981 and 2000. It left investors empty handed. In the decade that followed, gold roared back with a 450% gain. That's what makes gold a market timing investment. We're not rewarded for holding on during the downturns, but the upturns are impressive. When timed right, the propensity to build wealth with gold exceeds that of stocks.

2012 – 2019

Like before, after gold outperforms, the S&P 500 takes a turn. Of notable interest is the fact that both gold and equities rise in 2019. At this point, the stock market was setting record highs amidst speculation that the ten-year bull run that kicked off after the 2007-2008 financial crisis would run out of steam—*which it did.* The rise in gold is viewed as a defensive play. Equities are still going higher, but smart investors are preparing themselves for the inevitable pullback.

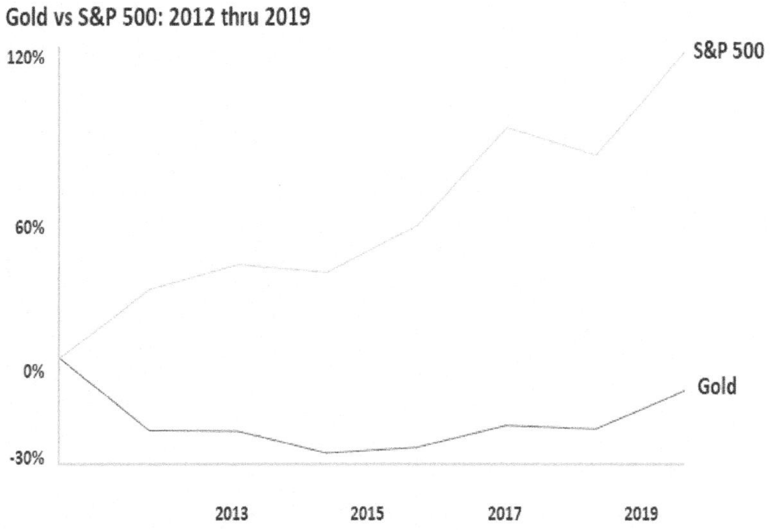

The back-and-forth between gold and equities over the past 49 years paints a very clear picture in terms of gold. It's not a buy-and-hold asset (unless it's being used as a portfolio hedge, in which case a 5% to 10% allocation is prudent). At times, the gold investor can earn generous returns while the S&P 500 moseys along. At other times, the S&P 500 outperforms while gold takes a breather. It's evident that healthy returns in gold are contingent on one's ability to time the market, and that a long-term buy-and-hold strategy can easily hold the investor back during consecutive decades. It would be misleading to draw the same conclusion about the S&P 500. The back-and-forth is evident, but when we view each asset class separately over the same 49-year period, it paints a vastly different picture.

Gold starts with a burst, spends two decades trending lower, advances quickly, falls rapidly, and then advances. Opportunities exist, but it does not exhibit the behavior that we look for in a buy-and-hold asset class. The fact that it doesn't pay a distribution further solidifies its position either as a modest hedge or a market timing tool.

Gold: 1971 thru 2019

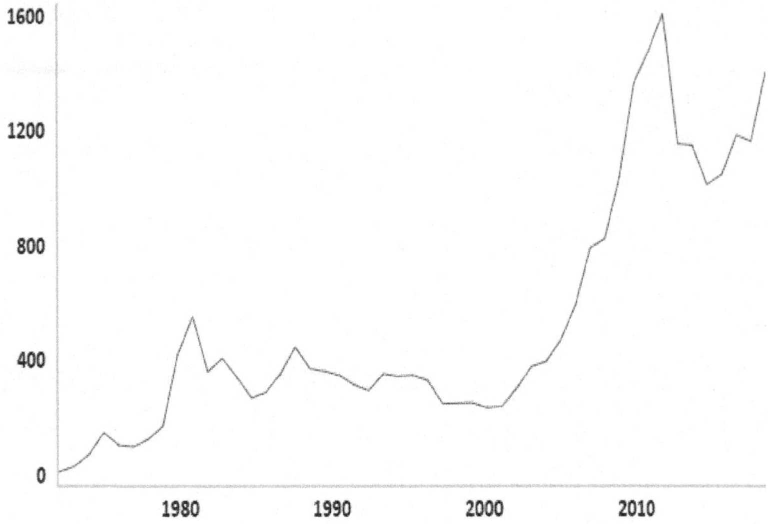

Shifting our attention to the S&P 500, we see that making money with a long-term buy-and-hold strategy is easy. Anyone can do it. All you have to do is transfer a prespecified percentage of your salary to a brokerage account each month, buy an index fund that tracks the S&P 500, set the account to automatically reinvest the dividends, and see things through during the bad times. Compared to gold, the bad times are relatively short and shallow. The S&P 500 gains more than twice the amount as gold during this period. When you consider the impact of reinvesting dividends for 49-years, the gains are even larger. Stocks win and gold loses, except for when gold provides huge returns over a short span of time. When this happens, stock investors tend to salivate over the missed opportunity.

S&P 500: 1971 thru 2019

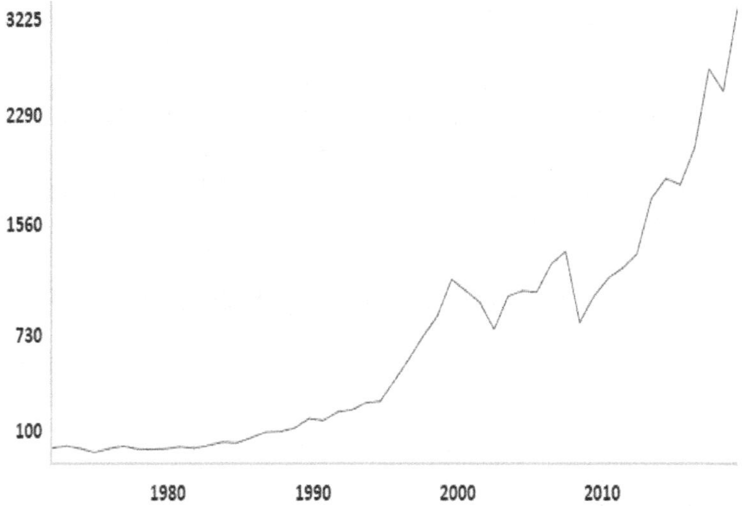

The disadvantage of holding gold for the long-haul is evident. Gold peaked in 1980 and didn't return to the $590 price level until 2006. Over this 26-year period, a hardworking and modestly aggressive investor could have easily set themselves up for a secure retirement, assuming they didn't over-weight their portfolio in favor of gold. The vast majority of investors put most of their reliance on stocks, and for good reason. Not only are the setbacks and lost years fewer and less severe, but the act of reinvesting dividends transforms the terms "setback" and "lost years" into misnomers. Dividends that get reinvested during "lost years" are put to work when stocks are priced at a discount. This enables investors to acquire more shares when prices are low, and thus earn more dividend income that will compound for the rest of their lives. Gold provides no such opportunity. When it's down, you either wait it out or invest in something else.

A Prelude to Strategy

Gold can provide amazing returns when the emotions of fear and greed cause the stock market to behave inefficiently. In hindsight, no one contests that stocks were overpriced at the turn of the century, yet investors continued pumping money into dot-com stocks until the bubble finally burst. The stock market peaked in March of 2000 and then spent the next two-and-a-half years falling. When it reached the bottom in September 2002, the S&P 500 still looked expensive. It easily could have fallen further, but it didn't.

Whether the stock market should be viewed as cheap or expensive can be measured by the P/E ratio:

P/E Ratio = Price / Earnings

Every stock has a P/E ratio. It's computed by taking the current price over the earnings from the previous year. A collective P/E ratio can also be computed for the greater market. The S&P 500, for example, has historically held an average P/E ratio of 16. When the ratio for the S&P 500 falls too far below 16, say around 12, stocks are considered cheap. When the ratio rises too far above 16, say around 20, stocks are considered expensive.

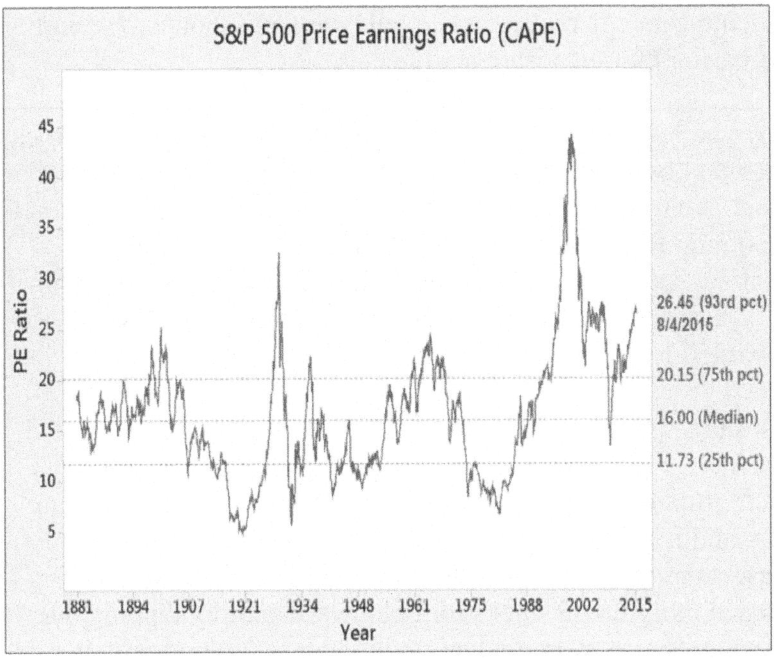

Before the dot-com bubble formed, the ratio shot up above 40. When the bubble burst, it didn't even fall below 20. Prices had been pushed so high that the market was able to undergo a crash without prices returning to a historically low level. In fact, it wouldn't fall below 16 until the 2007-2008 financial crisis, at which point it hovered just above 12. The investor who acknowledged that stocks were still expensive after the dot-com bubble burst and maintained, or even increased, their exposure to gold did quite well.

It's easy to analyze stock market crashes in hindsight. It's easy to say that stocks were expensive and a shift to gold was prudent. But when stocks are expensive yet continue to rise (and pay dividends) for upwards of five years before the next crash, how easy is it to maintain that lucrative position in gold? How does the gold investor know when to buy? And how do they know when to get out? I'll answer these questions in more detail in coming chapters. For now, it's sufficient to say that it's really easy to tell when the stock market is overpriced, which means it's really easy to tell when one should *first* start increasing their exposure to gold.

An experienced investor will tell you that just because the stock market is overpriced doesn't mean it's going to correct anytime soon. An overpriced market has the propensity to spend years becoming even more overpriced before it eventually falls. That's what happened between 2002 and 2007. Investors had five years to increase their exposure to gold, and they were rewarded for doing so.

Does this mean we should dump all our stocks in favor of gold when P/E ratios start to look expensive? *Absolutely not.* We could miss out on some really big stock market gains by doing that, and it could be years before the stock market falls and presents us with an opportunity to buy back in at a discount. Instead of dumping stocks for gold, we'll start by dipping our toes in the gold market when stocks start to look pricey. We might do this when the market first shows a P/E ratio above 20, or we might let it go a bit higher first. Then, as the stock market continues to ascend, we gradually increase our exposure to gold as we decrease our exposure to stocks. If other gold investors agree that stocks look expensive, they'll start doing the same. At this point in the cycle it's possible for stocks and gold to move in tandem—that is, both markets will move higher simultaneously. When the stock market eventually corrects, there will be panic selling, and this panic selling has a tendency to spread into other markets. Investors that hold leveraged positions receive margin calls, and many of them will be forced to sell unrelated assets. It creates a domino effect that's noticeable but short-lived. Once the margin calls are covered, markets again move freely.

While gold is viewed as a safe haven, it often succumbs to the residual effect of panic selling in the stock market. It tends to recover much faster and will provide strong returns as the stock market struggles to form a bottom and find direction. This happened in early 2000 when the dot-com bubble burst. It happened again during the 2007-2008 financial crisis, and then again in March 2020 when the coronavirus pandemic swept across the globe.

This is a very noticeable and recurrent pattern. When the stock market crashes, gold falls, which creates a short yet noticeable buy-in opportunity. Then gold takes off and provides stellar returns. The pattern is so noticeable and recurrent that it's difficult to ignore. It's also so infrequent that the opportunities to cash in on it are limited. Over the past 20 years, the opportunity has arisen on three separate occasions.

The overarching difference between stocks and gold is that the stock market exhibits an upward trend littered with periodic setbacks, while the behavior of gold is unpredictable until we enter an economic environment that will lead to high inflation. When this happens, the behavior of gold becomes very predictable—*it starts its ascent when fear of inflation is on the horizon, then goes up quickly when high inflation sets in.*

In Chapter 7, we'll dive deeper into the signals that indicate buy-in opportunities. For now, it's important to understand that gold and stocks exhibit different behavior, and the periods during which gold outperforms are typically shorter yet fiercer than the periods during which stocks outperform.

I'm a firm believer in holding the S&P 500 through all stages of the economic cycle. While setbacks and periods of stagnation will be encountered, a bear market in stocks is nothing more than an opportunity to buy more. The lost decade that stocks experienced at the turn of the century is mild compared to the back-to-back lost decades that gold experienced during the 1980s and 1990s.

At times, the forecast for gold can be grim. If I've done my job adequately, the only reasons you would buy gold and just sit on it is (1) for use as a modest portfolio hedge of no more than 10%, and (2) as an insurance policy rather than an investment.

In the event that our financial system collapses, gold is expected to maintain its value. Our fiat currency could conceivably be rendered worthless. If you're trying to build long-term wealth, the stock market is a more reliable asset class. If you want to build wealth quickly, gold has a history of providing great opportunities, but they can't be forced. You have to take them when they're available and focus on other asset classes when they're not.

Chapter 3: Why?

The question every investor should be asking is, *Why?* This isn't true just for gold, but for every investment. Before you acquire any type of investment you should understand why it's a good investment. If we dive deeper into this rationale, you shouldn't make an investment unless you truly understand how the investment works. In other words, how does it make money? Before you buy a stock, you should understand how the company earns a profit. You should also understand why they're expected to earn more than the competition. If you're a dividend investor, take time to understand how they've managed to increase their dividend each year for the past 35-or-so years. Whatever your reason for buying a stock, make sure you understand how the *why* behind your selection works. Before you invest in a bond, make sure you understand *why* the borrower is expected to pay off the debt. Before you invest in rental real estate, make sure you understand *why* there is a demand among renters for the property. It would be foolish to buy gold without understanding *why* the price of gold is expected to rise. If it's not expected to rise, then it's time to make a different investment.

Gold has many proponents. Ray Dalio is a firm believer in gold. Mike Maloney has built a celebrity around himself due to his knowledge of gold and advocacy of the asset class when the *why* is compelling. Kevin O'Leary allocates 5% of his portfolio to gold and loves the effect of rebalancing between gold and other asset classes. For him, the hedge is the *why*. He understands the science of investing in gold.

Most people think of Bill Gates as an entrepreneur, not an investor, but he also has plenty of investment experience. Gates makes the keen observation that gold as an investment is "psychological". Nothing drives demand other than a desire for gold. It's the fact that other investors share this desire that enables us to profit from a rising gold market. For Gates, the *why* rests in the ability of others to identify a *why*. When they do, that's his *why*.

George Soros is the classic example of an investor who understands the art of investing in gold. At times, Soros has been extremely bearish on gold, previously referring to gold as "the ultimate bubble" and mocking investors who bought bullion rather than stocks and bonds. Notwithstanding, in May 2017, Soros invested $123 million in the SPDR Gold Shares Trust (GLD). The trust rose 40% in the three-year period that followed. When Soros didn't have a *why*, he was bearish. When the landscape changed and the *why* became apparent, he changed his stance on gold and made a lot of money.

Those who have never seen a *why* for gold are often viewed as "permanent" bears, but their permanence has the propensity to change. Warren Buffet is a notable example. His reason for having been a "permanent" bear is perfectly rational. Gold just sits there. *That's it.* It doesn't produce anything and it doesn't pay a distribution. If instead of buying gold you bought farmland, you could grow vegetables on the farm, sell the vegetables, use the proceeds to buy more farmland, and you'd still have all of your original investment. Stocks pay dividends. You can use the dividends to buy more stocks, and like farmland, you still have your original investment. You can't do the same with gold. Buffet has stated many times that he doesn't want assets that just sit there; he wants assets that produce something. When gold declines in value, this sentiment is like gospel. But we can't ignore those short spans of time when gold provides massive returns while everything else continues to produce at a painfully slow pace. Gold increased 1300% in the 1970s while the S&P increased 47.33%. The dividends that stock investors earned didn't come anywhere close to patching the difference.

Warren Buffett is a value investor. His strategy relies on his ability to identify assets selling for less than their intrinsic value. If you want to know what a stock is worth—not what it's selling for, but what it's worth—you make projections about the company's future earnings and then discount those earnings back to present value. The present value is what the company is worth. If it's selling for less than that, then it's an investment that Warren Buffett might consider. Gold has no earnings, which makes intrinsic value incredibly difficult to calculate. But that doesn't mean gold never sells at a discount. It's just that the discounts are difficult to identify.

Stocks trade in a competitive environment where new companies can step up to the plate and steal market share from existing companies. In order to earn above-average returns on the stock market, the investor must not only identify companies that are going to outperform the competition, but also get in on those stocks while they're still priced below their intrinsic value. Gold doesn't compete with companies. It has a long history of competing with fiat currencies and is just now beginning to compete with cryptocurrencies. The intrinsic value of a fiat currency is easy to calculate—*it's zero*. Fiat currency doesn't pay a distribution and it loses value when more is printed—*eventually, the value of one U.S. dollar will be very, very close to zero*. In theory, the intrinsic value of gold is constant. It doesn't go up or down. It's the amount of fiat currency needed to buy gold that changes. Gold is still gold, just like coffee is still coffee. Cryptocurrencies present an interesting dynamic to this comparison. As we'll discuss in Chapter 10, cryptocurrencies and gold have a lot in common. If the supply of a cryptocurrency is finite, then we should expect its intrinsic value to be constant, just like gold. The number of U.S. dollars needed to buy one Bitcoin keeps changing, but Bitcoin is still Bitcoin, just like coffee is still coffee and gold is still gold, right? *Well, maybe.* What gold has that cryptocurrencies still needs to establish is a long history of acceptance. The verdict on cryptocurrencies is still out. It's unlikely that every cryptocurrency on the market is going to gain acceptance. Efforts to predict which one(s) will succeed is still a matter of speculation. For this reason, I'll argue that the intrinsic value of a cryptocurrency is even harder to calculate than that of gold.

At one end of the spectrum we have stocks, where the intrinsic value can be quite high because companies can conceivably provide infinite value. At the other end of the spectrum we have fiat currency, which is a medium of exchange that's doomed from the beginning because we expect more of the currency to be printed. Then we have cryptocurrencies, which is a medium of exchange that's still fighting for acceptance. In the middle of all this madness is gold. We expect the intrinsic value to be constant because there's a finite supply. The only thing that's expected to change is gold's worth when measured against other assets whose value isn't constant. Companies compete, they expand, they merge, they implode, they do all sorts of things. There's enough growth that a broad market investment is a safe bet over the long-term. You can buy in at any time and just go along for the ride. The stock investor who tries to do better than this by picking his own stocks has to contend with two additional questions: *Who?* and *When?* The game is now more challenging. The investor must identify which companies to invest in, and then decide if now is the time to invest. When both of these pieces come together, they have their *why*.

The gold investor is playing a different game. It's more challenging than simply buying into the market at any time, but less challenging than picking individual stocks. There's no *who* to contend with. Gold is gold. Instead, it's purely a question of *when*. With gold there's no risk of making your investment in the wrong company. Gold isn't going to go bankrupt, lose market share, or stop paying its dividend. Gold is completely tangible. You own it. It's not a promise to pay interest or deliver a good at some specified date in the future. It's not going to default on you. When you buy gold, you get gold. It's that simple. Aside from the risk of being scammed with fool's gold, there's little risk in picking the wrong gold like there is with investing in the wrong company (Enron, for example).

The *why* behind gold is the same as the *when*. *When* and *why* can we expect gold to increase in price. We can't answer one without answering the other. In essence, the art of investing in gold is narrowed down to a single question. We have the luxury of only having to focus on the entry and exit points, but that doesn't mean gold is an easy asset class to time. A bull run in the stock market can last for years. At the time of writing, an 11-year bull run that lasted from March 2009 through March 2020 has just come to an end. The average stock investor didn't have to be a market-timing genius in order to make money during the past decade. They simply had to make an investment. Gold is different. The bull runs are much shorter, but the gains have the propensity to be significantly larger. Gold is an asset class that's utilized by skilled investors to reap large returns during finite and somewhat erratic intervals. Gold works wonders during periods of high inflation. That's where the wealth transfer comes into play. When inflation is high, fiat currencies lose tremendous value, but the value of gold remains constant. It can then be traded for significantly more dollars as a result of high inflation. It's just a matter of timing.

The "*why now?*" of gold is important, but it's not the only reason why someone might invest in gold. Just for a minute, let's not focus on market timing and the expectation of high returns, but instead turn our attention to anonymity. Gold can be stored without a paper trail. The same can't be said of your brokerage account, savings account, retirement plan, or social security benefits. Gold, in this respect, is different. I won't get into the different reasons that an investor might desire anonymity, but I can say this, the gold that's buried in your back yard is off the charts. We know that there are 190,000 tons of gold in circulation, but we have no idea where all of it is. We don't know how much our neighbor does or doesn't have . . . *and neither does the government*. Again, it's not my place to come up with reasons why anonymity is desirable, but if you're looking to make an anonymous investment, the precious metals market is one place you can look.

Another notable *why* is that gold serves as the reserve currency should the financial system ever need reset. This might seem like an unlikely reason to buy gold, but it deserves our attention nonetheless. We accept the world and our financial system for what it is, but every financial system to date, other than our current financial system, has failed. The Byzantine empire lasted 900 years, but it eventually collapsed and the financial system needed reset. Granted, times have changed and technologies have advanced, but during that 900-year period, how many people thought the system was going to collapse? And what percent of them were still around when it did collapse? I present this as food for thought. A financial system collapse is a distinct possibility. Will we be around when it happens? Will the heirs that we bequeath our gold to be around when it happens? Your guess is as good as mine. The real point I want to make is that the *why* behind gold can change. No financial market is static; there's constant evolution. Currencies used to be backed by their weight in gold, and now gold is used to hedge against a decline in the purchasing power of said currencies. Currencies at one time were circulated predominately by governments, and now we're dealing with cryptocurrencies and struggling to decipher the role that they should play, both as an investment and as a medium of exchange.

There's a host of global economic factors that influence the price of gold, with high inflation having the strongest impact. The question isn't simply a matter of *why gold?* It's a matter of *why now?* And at other times, *why not now?* Yes, it's a market timing question, but at the same time, it's much, much more. Why does a diversified portfolio need to be hedged with gold? Why do prophets of doom and gloom bury gold in their back yard? Why do most central banks wait until the fear of recession sets in to buy more gold? The answers aren't just contingent on where the market is headed next, but on the very notion that our financial infrastructure is prone to vulnerabilities. Lehman Brothers and Bear Sterns both closed shop during the 2007-2008 financial crisis because of their exposure to toxic assets. If they had lowered their exposure to mortgage-backed securities and collateralized debt obligations and increased their exposure to gold, they would both still be operating today. But, during the majority of the economic cycle, gold isn't sexy. It doesn't pay dividends or provide huge returns. The payoff typically comes when other securities fail. Most investment banks aren't bullish on gold. As Warren Buffett has pointed out, gold doesn't do anything. Its appeal is limited to specific intervals in the economic cycle, while the returns that banks were earning on toxic derivatives were expected to persist indefinitely. Perhaps this train of thought needs to change.

Warren Buffett might be the most famous of all outspoken gold bears, but just like George Soros, he eventually saw the light glimmering at the end of the tunnel. It was announced on August 14, 2020 that Warren Buffett had assumed a large position of Barrick Gold Corporation (GOLD). A gold miner is different than gold. It's a company. Its value isn't just dependent on the spot price of gold, but also on how efficiently the company is run. In addition to mining gold, Barrick Gold also mines copper. They pay a dividend that yields 1.18%, which is impressive for a gold mining company. It will allow Buffett to reinvest the distribution as he maintains his initial investment. All this aside, the price that a gold mining stock sells for is strongly correlated to the spot price of gold. We'll see in Chapter 9 that gold mining stocks function as a leveraged position in gold. The upside is like greed on steroids, but the downside is devastating. This move by Buffett is an extremely bullish stance in favor of gold. Even more interesting is the fact that Buffett simultaneously dumped his bank stocks. The Sage of Omaha has a cult following. Investors not only watch his every move, they also have a tendency to imitate his positions. When Buffett buys, the herd will follow suit and push the price higher. Sometimes the *why* is contingent solely on economic indicators. At other times, the *why* is just a factor of what the smart money is doing. When it comes to watching the smart money, investors like Ray Dalio, Kevin O'Leary, Mike

Maloney, George Soros, and Warren Buffett are leading the game.

Chapter 4: How to Buy (and Store)

Let's jump into the most fundamental aspect of investing in gold—*how to buy*. It's a complicated subject that deserves your time and attention up front. Once you understand the pros and cons of investing in different forms of gold—and yes, there are more than most people realize—your attention will then shift from deciding how to buy to focusing on when to buy.

Gold is unique in that it can be purchased a variety of different ways, yet at the end of the day, an investment in gold is an investment in gold. The typical stock investor doesn't spend much time contemplating how they plan to make their purchase—*they use a broker, that's it.* But they do spend a lot of time deciding which stocks to buy. The gold investor, on the other hand, already knows what they want to invest in—*they want gold.* But how the gold is bought and stored makes a difference. The options are many. We can buy bullion bars, either from a dealer or a vaulting service. We can invest in gold coins and store them right in our home. We might buy jewelry, too. Or we can invest in an ETF that holds gold in trust at a major bank. If we're really adventurous, we might even dabble in the options market.

There are different ways to buy gold, and we'll see that the methods of buying and storing gold make a difference, but these differences are minor compared to the differences between a winning stock and a losing stock. At the end of the day, we're invested in gold. When the spot price of gold goes up, bars, coins, jewelry, ETFs, and call options all tend to rise in equal proportions. But if the financial system that you bought gold to protect yourself against actually unfolds, how you bought and stored your gold makes all the difference in the world. An ETF could easily be rendered worthless. The resale price of the bars you keep locked in a safe inside your home might skyrocket (but so too will the prospects of getting robbed).

A true gold buff will tell you that taking physical possession of gold is the only way to invest. Gold isn't just a hedge against high inflation and the mass printing of fiat currencies, it's also a hedge against complete financial Armageddon. You can't have your gold locked up in a safety deposit box when this happens, because what you're protecting yourself against is the failure of the institution that houses the safety deposit box. In order for gold to provide true protection against all failures, it needs to be in your home. You can lock it in your own personal safe or even bury it in your back yard. As long as you have access to gold in the event of a financial emergency, you're covered. I respect this perspective, but I also think it's a bit antiquated. If we ever reach the point where the only store of value is the bullion we have hidden in our homes, I question how and with whom we will use said bullion to barter. I also wonder if canned beans will hold greater value.

Even if the financial system doesn't collapse during our lifetime, there's no doubt that the system is going to change. Just look at what blockchain has the potential to do to the banking industry. Instead of each bank holding a centralized ledger that's subject to audit, transactions can now take place on a decentralized ledger that's completely transparent. Blockchain technology has the potential to greatly reduce fraud. It also makes our mistakes really difficult to correct. Innovations are great as long as we're prepared for the changes that ensue. Once an innovation is complete, all it needs is acceptance.

We should expect the financial system to be tested at least every thirty to forty years. The 2007-2008 financial crisis is a great example. The banking industry went through numerous changes and money was unofficially stolen. Those who invested in gold, be it bullion, coins, jewelry, or ETFs, recognized large gains while the rest of the world lost faith not only in their investments, but in the institutions that housed their investments.

There's additional risk involved when you don't take physical possession of an investment. Sometimes this risk is unavoidable and sometimes it's desirable. The easiest way to increase your returns is to increase your exposure to risk. If you find a way to combine different asset classes in such a way that the return increases while the risk is mitigated, even better. No two investors are alike. We subscribe to different strategies and we tweak these strategies based on our own idiosyncrasies. When it comes to investing in gold, how we buy and store the gold is as much a factor of our strategy as it is a factor of what we're protecting ourselves against.

The ETF is the most convenient vehicle we have for gaining exposure to a vast array of securities, but that doesn't mean the nature of an ETF isn't risky. Do we ever really know if the ETF actually holds the assets they claim to hold? And should convenience be the driving force behind the decision of how we invest in gold? With real estate, it's impossible for the average investor to gain adequate diversification by taking physical possession of property. I certainly can't afford to buy property in every state, but I can invest in an ETF that provides exposure to the entire domestic real estate market (and even markets abroad, if I want). The ETF solves the diversification problem. But with gold, it's actually quite easy to possess the commodity. There's limited room to diversify within the gold market. Instead, gold is a commodity that investors add to their portfolio in an effort to diversify across different markets. The ETF doesn't reduce risk, but rather, increases the probability that you've invested in a derivative when you thought you were buying the actual commodity. It pays to read the prospectus and understand the specific asset type that the ETF provides exposure to. Some gold ETFs hold nothing but bullion. Others hold a combination of bullion and options. Still others hold only the options.

There are many different ways to buy and store gold. Being aware of the different options is important, but understanding the advantages and disadvantages of each option is paramount. Let's have a look.

Bullion

Investors who want to take physical possession of their holding are advised to buy gold bullion. Technically, the word bullion refers to any high purity form of gold, including bars, ingots, or coins, but the term is most commonly associated with gold bars. When taking physical possession of gold, the decision between buying bars and coins is important. Gold bars tend to be the bullion of choice for investors. Gold coins appeal to collectors and have the potential to provide what is known as numismatic value. While gold in any form is considered rare, certain coins are more sought after than others, which adds additional complexity to the concept of rarity.

Gold bars trade at a lower price per ounce. When buying bullion, you'll get more bang for your buck with bars than you will with coins or jewelry. Bars don't require much in the way of craftsmanship. Investors typically pay a small premium above the spot price. Coins, on the other hand, tend to require the most craftsmanship. As a result, collectors are going to pay a higher premium. Jewelry is even worse. Here, the premium isn't necessarily the result of detailed craftsmanship, but a factor that's specific to the source of the demand. There are social customs that require couples to exchange rings. The jewelers know this. That's why the premium on gold jewelry is astronomical compared to both bars and coins. From an investment perspective, gold bars are the low-cost alternative that most serious investors choose.

The size of gold bars ranges from 1 gram to 400 ounces. If you're in a position to acquire a 400-ounce bar of gold, more power to you, but bullion in this form is most commonly acquired by central banks, the International Monetary Fund, ETFs, and extremely wealthy investors. Most individuals acquire significantly smaller bars.

Even with gold bars, the premium isn't static. In most cases, the smaller the bar, the higher the premium per ounce. Premiums can range from 1% to 10%, all depending on the size of the bar, the quality of the gold, and the condition of the market. When demand is high, premiums tend to inch higher. The premium also increases according to the purity. Just as there are both investment and non-investment grade bonds, the gold market offers both investment and non-investment grade gold. Investment grade gold comes from a reputable mint or a refinery and has purity of 99.5% or higher. Where a bond investor might add non-investment grade bonds (known as junk bonds) to their portfolio in order to increase their yield, gold investors are advised to avoid non-investment grade gold. Given that gold doesn't pay interest or any form of distribution, there's no incentive to buy non-investment grade. If you do, unloading the investment could be a challenge.

An investor looking to pay the lowest premium will naturally buy the largest bar he can afford, rather than buying several smaller bars. But that doesn't mean buying the largest bar possible is always the way to go. If you intend to sell your holdings in shifts as the market advances, buying several smaller bars provides a notable advantage. If you're allocating a specific percent of your portfolio to gold, smaller bars provide another advantage. The amount that you'll buy and sell to rebalance the portfolio depends on the performance of your holdings. If precision is important, keep it small. Smaller bars enable you to sell just a little if that's what you need. An ETF is even more convenient for this purpose. If gold is being held strictly as a hedge against other asset classes, like stocks, bonds, and real estate, rather than as a hedge against the failure of the financial system, a gold ETF is the easiest way to get the job done. As long as you have a device in hand, shares can be bought and sold in just a few clicks. That doesn't mean gold bullion isn't a liquid asset. It just means that it might take a couple hours, rather than a few clicks, to turn your bullion into cash.

A reputable dealer should be able to buy your bullion at any time (assuming it's investment grade gold from a recognized refinery). Your bars—whether they're in a safety deposit box at the bank, at home in a safe, or buried in your back yard—are liquid. As long as you have access to the gold, it can be redeemed.

If you're a new investor, finding a reputable dealer is your first task. Gold dealers have a wealth of experience and they can spot a newbie before he's halfway through the door. Just as you would with any other business, look for dealers with strong customer ratings. You'll want to rely on reviews posted to websites that aren't maintained by the dealer. Gold isn't cheap. Customers who have a bad experience are likely to complain. A strong Better Business Bureau rating is also a plus.

A reputable dealer should be able to tell you what your gold is worth, even if no transaction takes place. They should also be able to make a firm offer that falls below the spot price by only a small discount. If the dealer tries to sell you appraisal services instead of making an offer, turn around and walk away. There are plenty of dealers who will voluntarily tell you what your gold is worth. These dealers are more interested in building and protecting their reputation than they are in taking advantage of a newbie. In the long run, these dealers are more successful.

When buying bullion, stick to dealers that have a published buy-back policy. This will make life so much easier when you're ready to sell. With a buy-back policy, you know how much your dealer is going to give you for the gold. It's generally expressed as a discount below the spot price. If you decide to shop around for a competitive redemption price, you know the exact number that other dealers need to beat. Sometimes you'll find a better price. Other times, you'll find that the best price you're going to get is listed in your dealer's buy-back policy. When this happens, you'll appreciate the benefit of only buying from dealers who publish their policy.

The premium and discount at which you buy and sell gold is the same concept as the bid/ask spread on stocks. The price that gold is currently selling for is the spot price. In order to earn a profit, dealers buy gold at a discount to the spot price and then sell it at a premium to the spot price. They're not taking advantage of customers by building reasonable discounts and premiums into their business model; these guys need to make a living too. It's only when the spread gets too wide that you should start looking elsewhere.

The spot price is easy to track. It's at the very top of the screen on marketwatch.com, along with quotes for the Dow Jones Industrial Average, the S&P 500, the Nasdaq, and oil. If you know the spot price going into a transaction, you're less likely to be taken advantage of.

You should only buy bullion with a recognized hallmark and proper stamping. The hallmark is essentially a certificate of purity. Gold is easier to sell when it has the hallmark of a reputable refinery. Without a hallmark, the resell opportunities are fewer. The purity can still be measured by an experienced dealer, and if the gold is going to be used to make jewelry, then there's no point in preserving the hallmark. But without a recognized hallmark, most dealers and investors won't be interested. Those who are will demand a larger discount. Valcambi Suisse, Johnson Matthey, Produits Artistiques Métaux Précieux, the Royal Canadian Mint, The Perth Mint of Australia, Argor Heraeussa, and Sunshine Mint are among the more reputable refiners in the world, but this list is far from exhaustive.

Coins

Before we discuss the intricacies of buying coins, let's first discuss why a lot of investors avoid coins altogether. As mentioned above, you'll pay a higher premium than you will for bars. This has a lot to do with the fact that coins are a crafted product rather than a pure commodity. They're collectables, which is great if you like to collect things. But gold coins aren't just collectables, they're expensive collectables. They're significantly more expensive than *most* baseball cards, but compared to collecting fine art, rare wines, and vintage Mustangs, it's still an affordable hobby. The ultimate goal is to sell your coins for more than the purchase price. This can present certain challenges. When we move from bars to coins, aspects such as age, rarity, and condition play an important role. It's just like collecting baseball cards. Most baseball cards are only worth as much as the cardboard that they're printed on, while rare cards of notable players demand a hefty premium. Just ask anyone who collected cards during the late 1980s and early 1990s. If they pulled a Ken Griffey Jr rookie card out of a pack of 1989 Upper Deck, then they have something of value. If they instead used their paper route money to build a complete set of 1989 Topps, then they have a collection of cardboard that isn't worth much of anything.

With gold coins, the resale value is more predictable because it fluctuates with the spot price of gold. An American Gold Eagle or Canadian Maple Leaf will sell at a noticeable premium. Your ability to resell coins that are both high quality and easily recognized is certain. Some coins have numismatic value and can sell for as much as 500 times the spot price of gold. Pre-1933 U.S. gold coins, for example, are highly cherished among collectors. To get one today, you'll likely pay an arm and a leg.

A true investor doesn't care about the collectability of coins. To them, the movement in the spot price of gold is all that matters, not the numismatic value of a specific coin. Investment grade gold is investment grade gold, period. But to a collector, not all coins are created equal. The American Gold Eagle, Canadian Maple Leaf, and Mexican Gold Peso are all readily available. The Rooster from France, on the other hand, is highly sought after and demands a higher premium. A low premium on a coin is indicative of low demand, which shouldn't be mistaken for a bargain. When you get in cheap on a collectable, you might find yourself holding it in perpetuity. Where a reputable bullion dealer will have a published buyback policy, the same does not apply to coin dealers. They only buy what they can easily resell, which might not be the coin you managed to procure at a low premium. If a gold coin looks like a bargain because it's selling for less than the spot price, the first thing you want to ask yourself is, *why?*

As you move from high quality coins down to the less sought-after (or even unrecognizable) coins, the odds continue to stack (no pun intended) against the collector. Some coins are like that Beanie Baby you're still holding onto because nobody on eBay wants it. And speaking of eBay, or any medium that connects buyers and sellers outside of an established dealer-customer relationship, these are great places to get ripped off. My advice is to only do business with reputable dealers and trusted investors that you've formed a relationship with. A lot of the gold for sale on eBay and other peer-to-peer exchanges isn't really gold. This applies to all forms of gold, not just coins. On top of that, eBay charges a commission, so in addition to dealing with premiums, you're also dealing with fees.

So if we know that the premium is higher, why would someone collect (or invest in) gold coins? The answer is that four syllable word I keep tossing around as though everyone knows what it means. Numismatic value refers to the fair market value of a coin based on the scarcity of the coin, its condition, supply, and demand. Where investment grade gold carries a uniform spot price, each coin carries a unique numismatic value. Some coins sell for less than the spot price of gold because the numismatic value is impaired by the condition of the coin. A heavily circulated coin that's soft and has accumulated a few nicks and scratches is going to sell for less than a scarcely circulated coin that's strong and in mint condition. The resale value depends on more than the spot price. This serves as an additional layer of complexity that a lot of investors don't want to deal with, but for a skilled coin collector, the added complexity is seen as an opportunity. The goal is to acquire coins where the numismatic value increases at a faster rate than the spot price of gold.

A highly skilled coin collector doesn't just understand gold as an investment, but also knows which coins to buy. When they spot a bargain, they know whether or not the coin is a good prospect for resale, and they also know that these bargains aren't found on eBay. Most likely, they frequent trade shows and they know every dealer in town. Collectors understand the concept of scarcity. Gold itself is scarce, but coins are a little different. When a new coin hits the market, there could be a sense of scarcity relative to other coins, as long as the mint doesn't keep making more. If they do, the scarcity will quickly dilute. In this regard, acquiring a coin that's expected to increase in numismatic value is a gamble. The mint could flood the market in order to meet demand, which makes the resale value of the coin, when compared to coins of equivalent weight and purity, lower.

It's common for experienced collectors to avoid a new coin release. Just like an initial public offering on the stock market, the price is likely to drop shortly after the release. An experienced collector waits for this to happen. They get a feel for how much more, if any, is going to be minted. Then they buy only if they believe the scarcity factor will work to their benefit.

Like bullion bars, gold coins are a physical asset. It's easy to take possession and store in your home. Coins are more expensive to insure if stored in your home instead of a safety deposit box. Coins also provide protection against a collapse of the financial system. Given that coins are relatively small, these assets will be handy to barter with should the financial system actually collapse.

The act of accumulating gold coins is referred to as stacking. If you didn't understand the previous pun, that's where it came from. As we've already discussed, not all gold coins are created equal. The thickness of the coin makes a difference. Some of the softer gold coins accumulate scratches, which makes them harder to sell. You might see other collectors take their coins out of the cases and toss them around like they're bulletproof, but it's really not a good idea. Think of them like baseball cards. If the coin is truly valuable, it should have its own case that it's never removed from. The less it's touched with human hands, the better.

Some collectors start with silver because it's less expensive than gold. An advantage to starting with silver is that mistakes are less costly when buying a lower-priced metal. After experience has been gained, you might decide to sell your silver and start buying gold.

Another approach is to make frequent purchases of smaller coins instead of saving up for a larger coin. Granted, you'll pay more in premiums along the way, but by making more frequent purchases in smaller increments, the collector reaps the benefit of dollar cost averaging. They buy a small coin each month regardless of what's happened to the spot price of gold. If the spot price keeps going up, then the larger coin that they're saving for keeps getting more expensive; it becomes a moving target, which is good for those who already own the coin, but not for you. If instead of saving for the coin you want, you make monthly investments in smaller coins, then the resale value of those coins will rise alongside the larger coin. It doesn't matter that you pay a higher premium per ounce for the smaller coins. Unlike the fiat currency that you use to buy coins, small coins are going to appreciate in tandem with large coins. Of course, there's no guarantee that the spot price of gold won't go down, in which case the resale value of your small coins takes a dip along with the price of the larger coin. That's fine, too. An advantage of making consistent purchases on a monthly basis is that you get in on the dips. Don't get frustrated when the market goes down; see it instead as an opportunity to buy more.

Smaller coins are less likely to be counterfeited. The profit margin on a small coin is smaller, so there's less incentive to counterfeit. On top of that, the detail on a small coin is more difficult to replicate. Counterfeiters usually stick to larger coins with higher profit margins because they're easier to replicate.

While many of the intricacies of investing in (or collecting) coins work against those who don't have the specialized knowledge to evaluate a coin's numismatic value, there are intermittent periods when holding coins enables even the most passive of coin collectors to earn a large return. During periods of fear when physical gold is in high demand, it's possible for coins to be out of stock with many dealers. This tends to happen when an unexpected yet relatively prolonged demand exceeds the rate at which coins are produced by the U.S. Mint. When this happens, the coins that are out of stock sell at a higher premium, which means collectors can demand a higher price for their holdings. It would be risky to base a strategy on identifying coins that you think the U.S. Mint will run out of. Instead, consider it a field day should you happen to hold one of these coins.

Jewelry

I'm going to keep this section short and sweet. For the most part, jewelry is not an investment, it's a consumable. A large position in jewelry should be reserved for those who've achieved notable success with their investments—or through other facets of life—and, dare I use such a word, want to adorn themselves with a bit of *bling*. Perhaps an investment in jewelry makes your significant other feel appreciated while enabling you to simultaneously feel as though you've made a wise investment. Jewelry can and does appreciate in value. But it's not the best asset class for the investor looking to keep fees and premiums low, strategize entry and exit points, and basically make the most of their investment. When inflation is high and gold is peaking, try telling your significant other that it's time to hawk that bracelet you gave her on your anniversary. I'd love to be a fly on the wall for that conversation.

We know that coin collectors pay a higher premium than bullion bar investors. The jewelry consumer pays an even higher premium. It's not that jewelry requires a higher degree of craftsmanship than gold coins (the detail on coins is more intricate than most jewelry), but more so that it's a different market with different properties of supply and demand. The demand is built into the fabric of our society. You can't follow traditional marriage customs without exchanging gold rings, but you can easily become an active investor without ever touching gold. As a result, the jewelry consumer gets skinned alive in terms of the premium, while the investor only pays a modest premium.

The reasons not to view jewelry as an investment are many. It costs more to insure. It's more likely to be fake or have enough copper and zinc added to it that it's not investment grade. And if you wear it out on the town, people will know you have it and it's more likely to be stolen. If you don't believe me, then I recommend reading *Confessions of a Master Jewel Thief* by Bill Mason. It's an extremely entertaining read. It will also make you think twice about how you invest in and store your jewels and precious metals. When we get to the section on investment strategy, the focus will be on the gold ETF. Granted, an ETF doesn't protect us against a financial system collapse, but with an ETF, you don't have to worry about someone like Bill Mason scaling a twenty-story building to steal jewelry out of the safe in your hotel room. You might laugh at this analogy, but thefts of this nature happen more frequently than the collapse of our financial system.

Those who own large amounts of jewelry tend to keep their most expensive items in safety deposit boxes. They might retrieve certain items on special occasions, but most of the time, their jewelry is locked for safe keeping. While the safety deposit box is likely maintained by a major bank, please note that the contents of the safety deposit box are not FDIC insured. It's the responsibility of the customer, not the bank, to insure their items.

Vaulting Service

Life is great when someone else does all the work. That's exactly what a vaulting service does. They take the load off your shoulders, in more ways than one. The services offered by different vaults aren't completely identical, but most reputable vaulting services enable you to buy and sell either with dealers on staff or through an established dealer relationship. They provide storage, monitoring, insurance, and delivery. Transactions can be executed from the comfort of your own home. It's not necessary to visit the location, though visitation is generally permitted.

A vaulting service is different than a safety deposit box, though many banks do hold themselves out as though the offer vaulting services. Be aware that there is a significant difference between services offered by banks and a legitimate vaulting service.

Security is the number one benefit of a vaulting service. These companies are subject to routine audits, so while you're not in possession of the gold and may actually never see the gold, you can rest assured that it's there and has been earmarked for your ownership.

Another benefit of vaulting services is the low cost of investing. Historically, individual investors have been at a disadvantage in the precious metals market because they buy and sell in such small quantities. Compared to a central bank or the International Monetary Fund, individuals are forced to pay higher premiums. A vaulting service mitigates this problem.

They buy in bulk on behalf of many individual investors and can therefore ensure that their customers get the lowest possible premium. It's similar to the concept of a discount broker for stocks. None of the individual account holders are able to go directly to an exchange and make transactions at a low cost; it's the discount broker that makes this possible. After stocks have been purchased, the discount broker holds them on your behalf. You can log into your account each day, monitor your holdings, see what they're worth, and you can sell whenever you want. A vaulting service does the exact same thing, except they're also tasked with taking physical possession, keeping the asset safe, and providing insurance. They also provide online trading platforms so all the investor has to do is buy and sell. Your gold is just a few clicks away.

It's important to only buy gold from vaults that keep the gold segregated. In other words, the gold that you buy should be kept in a bin that's separate from gold that belongs to other customers. If you decide to visit the vault, they will be able to show you your bin and you will know which specific bars of gold are yours. Not all vaults segregate their gold. Some vaults keep all of their gold together and simply sell a stake in the gold. If you go this route, you're not really buying gold, but are instead buying a piece of paper that represents your right in a storage of gold. It's similar to when the United States was on the gold standard. There was currency (pieces of paper) in circulation and there was gold in reserve, but no matter how hard they tried, the paper in circulation did not reconcile to the amount of gold in reserve. The problem this causes is obvious. It's not as severe as the problem of printing dollars at an irresponsible rate, but a problem of the same nature nonetheless. A vaulting service that keeps all of its gold together and simply sells you a stake in the gold should be avoided. Instead, stick to a vaulting service that keeps *your* gold segregated. When gold is segregated, the amount in storage should never deviate from the amount that the customer owns. Segregated gold comes at a slightly higher premium, but the peace of mind is worth the extra cost.

Some investors opt for vaulting services outside of their home country. They look for vaults in politically stable countries with strong property rights, a healthy economy, and solid military defense. The most important consideration is whether the country has a history of seizing assets. Some locations provide more anonymity than others. Tax treatment is also a consideration. Historically, Switzerland, Singapore, and Hong Kong have been popular locations. Most vaults offer delivery services should the investor decide to take physical possession, but a lot of investors buy and sell gold from vaulting services in different countries without taking physical possession or visiting the vault. Working with a vaulting service that has a good reputation is crucial.

Regardless of location, the ability to buy and sell within the facility is what makes these services so convenient. Instead of going to the bank, retrieving gold from a safety deposit box and then transporting it yourself to a gold dealership, all transactions take place right there at the vault, and you don't even have to be present to facilitate the transaction. In other words, a good vaulting service doesn't just keep the asset safe, it also provides liquidity.

A growing number of vaults are starting to accept payment in Bitcoin and other cryptocurrencies. Some are even expanding their services so that customers can trade and invest in cryptocurrencies. This makes sense, because cryptocurrencies that have a fixed quantity function more like gold than a fiat currency.

When you store gold with a vaulting service, you protect yourself from inflation and all the other ripples of the economic cycle that gold protects against. If the vaulting service is independent from the banking industry, you also protect yourself from the risk of a financial system collapse. If the "too big to fail" banks fail, you should still be able to access your gold.

The downside to a vaulting service is that it's more difficult to rebalance your portfolio against assets held in your brokerage account. Instead of simply executing a trade, there's money to be transferred. It's not an incredibly onerous or lengthy process, but it can take several days, particularly if the vaulting service is located in a foreign country. Markets can move in that time. If gold has gone up and stocks have gone down, the process of rebalancing will force you to sell some of your gold in order to buy more stocks. It might take a few days to sell gold through your vaulting service and then have the proceeds transferred to your brokerage account. In that time, stocks could move higher, which will dilute the benefit of rebalancing. If you hold a gold ETF in your brokerage account along with ETFs that hold stocks, bonds, and real estate, all of your asset classes can be rebalanced in a matter of minutes, and you don't have to worry about markets moving against you as you transfer funds.

Banks

Let's say that for whatever reason, you don't utilize a vaulting service. Instead, you buy and sell with local dealers, which means you take physical possession. You might keep some in your home, but this makes you susceptible to burglary and it's more expensive to insure, so the amount stored at home is modest at best. You want the majority of your holdings locked up at a remote location. It helps you sleep at night and makes your home feel like an actual home, not a fortress of solitude. So you take your bullion, your coins, and your jewelry, you open a safety deposit box at your local bank, and you lock them up for safe keeping.

Now, let's think about what happened in 2007-2008. The subprime mortgage bubble burst and a whole slew of banks filed for bankruptcy. Lehman Brothers and Bear Stearns both closed their doors in spite of the Emergency Economic

Stabilization Act having created a $700 billion trust to help relieve banks of toxic assets. *The taxpayers were peeved.* We felt betrayed. Financial institutions that we rely on to hold our assets for safekeeping had fallen down a rabbit hole of greed and corruption. It made a lot of people stop and ask the question, what happens to my assets if the holding institution ceases to exist? Deposits held at a bank are FDIC insured, right? Well, some of them are. Your checking, savings, and IRA accounts are insured up to $250,000 by the FDIC. The SIPC insures up to $500,000 in brokerage funds that go missing. Safety deposit boxes are different. Unlike a vaulting service, the bank isn't going to offer insurance. You have to find that on your own. Typically, gold stored in a safety deposit box is cheaper to insure than gold stored in your home, but it's still more expensive than gold stored with a vaulting service. That's because the vaulting service acquires insurance for many gold investors, and is therefore in a better position to negotiate.

In the event that the banking system collapses, a safety deposit box is one of the worst places to have your assets stored. You may or may not be able to access the safety deposit box and the problem could culminate in a lengthy dispute with the insurance company. If things are so bad that banks are closing their doors, it means there's a need for liquidity, and assets held in a safety deposit box are far from liquid under this scenario.

If you like having a portion of your gold locked up in close proximity, go ahead and store some of it in a safety deposit box. Under normal circumstances, you'll be able to access the gold at any time during regular banking hours. This advantage aside, a vaulting service offers more benefits at a lower cost. Most serious gold investors prefer a vaulting service.

When we get to Chapter 7, we'll discuss economic indicators that signal when to buy and sell gold. It's interesting to watch the volume of gold being bought and sold because it says a lot about investor sentiment. When gold demand picks up, people are worried about inflation. This is a telling signal, but even more telling is the demand for specific types of gold. When the demand for physical gold, including bullion and coins, outpaces the demand for ETFs, futures, and even gold mining stocks, it likewise means that people are worried. When an increase in demand for physical gold isn't coupled with an increase in demand for safety deposit boxes, it's a sign that investors are worried about the solvency of the banking industry.

Safety deposit boxes offer some advantages to the buy-and-hold investor looking to take physical possession. If your goal is to profit from fluctuations in the spot price of gold, rather than protect yourself from global catastrophe, the gold ETF is a better instrument.

ETF

This section is going to stomp all over conventional wisdom. As the prophets of doom and gloom keep saying, if you don't take physical possession of your gold, then you're not truly protected against every single possible disaster that could conceivably happen to the global financial system. That's okay, because the drawbacks of taking physical possession hit you where it hurts the most; *in your wallet*.

It costs money to store gold. It costs money to insure gold. If the gold is in your home, it costs even more to insure. This is money that could be invested in more gold. Or you could spread the money across other asset classes. Whatever the case, it's money that could be working for you. There is, of course, a risk in letting this money work for you, and that's the risk that everything else fails except for physical gold. It's unlikely, but not impossible. As I mentioned above, should things ever get so bad that the only real money left is the gold stored in your home, a can of beans is likely to hold greater value. There are also a lot of people who would rather have ample reserves of coffee.

Let's move on. We understand why physical gold provides additional protection. Now we're going to focus on the most convenient form of gold, and not surprisingly, the least likely to save you during a financial system collapse. I'm talking about exchange traded funds (ETFs). You buy and sell them through your discount broker (or full-service broker, if you're inclined to pay steep commissions) just as you would a share stock. Once you own an ETF, it's displayed in your brokerage account along with all of your other holdings. It's also really easy to trade back and forth between different ETFs.

As we progress into the strategies section, the ETF is going to be our weapon of choice. An ETF can hold virtually any asset class, ranging from stocks, bonds, real estate, and even cryptocurrencies. They also make ETFs that hold commodities, including gold.

The ETF is a convenient instrument, but it's not a perfect instrument; it is, in fact, very flawed. My goal for this section is to give you an understanding of the advantages and disadvantages that accompany the various methods of buying and storing gold. When it comes to the ETF, convenience is the quintessential advantage. Whatever transaction you want to make, it's literally a few clicks away. You can even buy and sell ETFs while riding the subway.

An ETF is essentially a derivative. You don't directly own the gold. Instead, you have an ownership interest in a trust, and if you buy the right gold ETF, the trust owns gold. Should something happen, you have liquidation rights. The gold might be held in trust, but the shares you own are backed by the gold, which is more than we can say for the U.S. dollar. Surprising, not all gold ETFs hold physical gold. Some gold ETFs hold options and futures contracts on gold. Or they might hold a combination of gold and gold contracts. If the ETF is a leveraged ETF—that is, the ETF is designed to provide either 2X or 3X the daily movement in the spot price of gold—then it's definitely holding contracts rather than gold. My advice is to stick with ETFs that actually invest in physical gold. The most recognized fund is the SPDR Gold Shares ETF (GLD). It has an average trading volume of 6.7 million shares per day. The iShares Gold Trust ETF (IAU) is another popular trust. It's sold in smaller increments and has an average trading volume of 16 million shares per day. If you want a leveraged investment, gold mining stocks can provide amplified gains and losses without exposing you to exotic derivatives. We'll discuss this further in Chapter 9. Two popular ETFs for gold mining stocks are the VanEck Vectors Gold Miners ETF (GDX) and the iShares MSCI Global Gold Miners ETF (RING).

The GLD stores gold in trust with HSBC, which is one of the largest bullion banks in the world. The IAU stores gold in trust with JP Morgan. While both banks are well-known and have the overhead to get the job done, it's fair to say that neither bank is free of negative publicity. In this day and age, few banks are. Nonetheless, the majority of the gold trading on the New York Stock Exchange is held with these institutions.

Investing in a gold ETF is similar to using a vaulting service that doesn't segregate its gold. You don't have specific bars earmarked to your investment. You also can't visit the gold, if that's important to you. This is a drawback. As Mike Maloney, the world's foremost guru on gold investing, has stated, "If you can't hold it, you don't own it."

The fact that shares trade continually on an exchange is an advantage. The worth of your holding is completely transparent and buyers are readily available. Additionally, gold ETFs are subject to audit, which provides assurance that the gold actually exists. If the ETF is registered with the SEC, as most are, then it should be eligible for SIPC insurance, which is one benefit of holding gold in an ETF over a safety deposit box or in your home. You should sleep well at night knowing that no one is going to break into your house and steal your ETFs. In this regard, the statement, "If you can't hold it, you don't own it," is more of a blessing than a curse.

The SPDR Gold Shares (GLD) is unique in that it allows wealthy investors to take physical possession, should they choose to. The trust permits shareholders with greater than 100,000 shares to exchange their holding for bullion. A wealthy investor might decide to invest in this ETF to hedge against rising inflation and then only request delivery of the gold when the outlook turns dreary and fear sets in. For most of us, acquiring 100,000 shares is out of reach. At the time of writing, the GLD trades at $190, meaning that 100,000 shares would cost $19 million.

In my opinion, an ETF that holds gold, not options or futures contracts, but actual gold, is a prudent instrument if your goal is to maintain a 5% to 10% portfolio hedge. It's also a convenient instrument for those seeking short-term protection against high inflation. If your goal is to build a gold reserve to protect yourself against a collapse of the financial system, the ETF isn't going to get the job done. Unless you have an extra $19 million lying around, there won't be anything to bury in your back yard.

Be aware that if the financial system does collapse, it's not just the gold ETF that's going down. All ETFs, including those that hold stocks, bonds, real estate, and commodities, could become worthless if the exchange they trade on ceases to exist. There might be some salvage value, but it's generally slim pickings after the lawyers get paid. For this reason, it pays to hold at least some physical assets, such as gold and real estate, at all times. Doing so doesn't mean you can't also fill your portfolio with ETFs.

A nice thing about the GLD and the IAU is that the bid/ask spread is narrow when compared to the premium paid for bullion. This is an often underrecognized benefit of an ETF. When buying and selling bullion from a dealer, it pays to do your homework and understand the premiums and discounts. In other words, the dealer likely knows more than the investor, and the transaction price is more likely to be in his favor than yours. This can be avoided by keeping yourself informed and building a relationship with a reputable dealer. But when you trade on an exchange, there's greater transparency. As long as the asset class has significant volume—which gold does—the combined behavior of every buyer and seller transacting on the exchange (all of whom are acting in their own self-interest) forces the asset to trade exceptionally close to the spot price. This doesn't mean that whenever you buy an ETF, you're making a smart investment. Rather, it means that once you've made the decision to buy or sell an ETF, the exchange ensures that you buy or sell at the going rate.

In addition to the bid/ask spread, ETF investors also pay a management fee. They don't all realize that they pay a management fee, but they do. The reason they might not know is because the holding is displayed in their brokerage account net of the fee. It doesn't get taken out separately. So if an ETF investor isn't paying attention, they could rack up some hefty fees without realizing it. In *Dividend Investing*, I discuss the importance of keeping fees low in order to increase your dividend income. ETFs that track an index (rather than being actively managed by a fund manager and a team of analysts) tend to have lower fees. Gold ETFs charge slightly higher fees than most stock ETFs, but still significantly less than most actively managed funds. The fee on a gold ETF is typically in the neighborhood of 0.4%.

Finally, we have the stop-loss order. This is a huge advantage of holding an ETF. A stop-loss is an order that executes after a stock or ETF falls below a specified threshold. It provides a certain level of protection. For example, if you buy the GLD at $182.45, you might enter a stop-loss order to sell if the price falls to $169.68. This limits the potential loss to 7%. If the economic environment changes and gold enters bear territory, you don't have to go along for the ride. You also don't have to make your sell decision during a correction when emotions might get in the way. You make this decision beforehand when you enter the stop-loss order. Now let's be optimists. Instead of the GLD falling back to $169.68, let's say it goes higher . . .

and then higher . . . and then higher still. You can increase the stop-loss order as this happens. If the GLD rises to $207.58, you might increase your stop-loss so that it executes when the price falls back to $193.05, or whatever amount you're comfortable with. Now instead of using the stop-loss to limit your potential loss, you're using it to limit the gains that you could potentially give back. The great thing about a stop-loss is that you don't have to sit in front of your computer all day. You can be out having a cup of coffee, stocking up on canned beans, or driving through the northern region of Michigan where cell phone reception fades away, and the order will still execute. The downside of a stop-loss is that you're not guaranteed that the order will be executed at the price you've set. When a stop-loss is triggered, the order automatically becomes a market order. That means it will be executed wherever the next trade takes place. If the security is falling fast, the next trade could take place at a lower price. But when you set a stop-loss on an ETF that's heavily traded, the chances of the trade executing at the same price that triggered the stop-loss are fairly certain.

Derivatives

In simple terms, a derivative is something that substitutes for something that it isn't. In financial terms, a derivative is an arrangement or instrument whose value derives from and is dependent on the value of an underlying asset. A good example is a futures contract that requires the holder to buy gold at a set price six months from the date of issue. The futures contract is not gold. Instead, it's a piece of paper that requires the holder to purchase gold. Another good example is a call option. Instead of being required to buy gold at a set price, the holder has the option to buy at a set price up until a specified date. If the price of gold goes up, the holder will either exercise the option or sell it for a gain. If it goes down, she'll have to sell the option for a loss.

The price that is agreed to in the contract is referred to as the strike price. With a call option, the value of the contract goes up as the spot price rises. When the spot price is above the strike price, the option is said to be in the money. The investor who buys a call option is therefore betting that the price of gold will go up.

Investors who dollar cost average into gold can earn a small return by selling call options. They know they are going to buy gold each month, so they attempt to profit at the same time by selling the option. If the option expires out of the money, they keep the revenue from selling the option and buy gold at the spot price (just as they would if they hadn't sold the option). If the spot price increases so that the contract is in the money, they'll be forced to sell some of their gold at a price that's below the spot price. They will continue to dollar cost average and also buy more gold at the spot price. In this situation, they might still come out ahead. They earned revenue from selling the call option. If the revenue exceeds the difference between the spot price and the strike price, they're better off for having sold the call option. If gold goes up so much that the difference between the spot price and the strike price exceeds the revenue, they'd have been better off not selling the call option. While this situation isn't ideal, the revenue still mitigates the damage. Over time, they typically come out ahead because it's only during the times when the spot price advances by more than the revenue collected that they actually lose money.

A put option is a contract that gives the holder the option to sell. In other words, they get to put it to the writer of the contract. The investor who buys a put is either betting that the spot price of gold will go down or is looking to protect gains that they've already earned on their investment. If the investor buys a put to protect her position in gold, it's referred to as a protective put. If she buys a put but isn't simultaneously invested in gold, it's referred to as a naked put. With puts, the spot price has to fall below the strike price in order for the contract to be in the money. If this happens, the holder will either sell the contract for a gain or exercise the option. If it doesn't, she'll have to sell the option for a loss.

A naked put is purely a gamble. The holder is bearish on gold and buys a put option in order to profit from the anticipated decline. A better use of a put is to hedge. A gold investor who has earned remarkable returns on gold but thinks the market has room to go higher will buy a protective put as insurance. If the market does go higher, she loses the amount that she paid for the put, but that's okay because she's still racking up gains on her gold. This should outweigh the cost of the put. In the event that gold doesn't move higher, but instead loses considerable ground, she can exercise the put option and sell at the strike price, which in this scenario is higher than where the spot price has fallen.

Another intricacy of derivatives is that they enable gold investors to apply leverage. An investor can buy call options for significantly less than the cost of gold, which enables them to essentially control large quantities of gold at a low cost. If the spot price of gold increases, the investor's return is multiplied. But if it goes down, they'll be forced to sell the contract at a loss.

Put options also enable the investor to apply leverage. It's cheaper to buy put options than to enter into a short position, say with an ETF. Both a put option and a short position in an ETF pay off when the spot price goes down, but with a put option, the returns are multiplied. If it goes up, the investor will sell the put option at a loss.

Leverage is a double-edged sword. While the upside potential is large, the downside potential can be damaging. For this reason, the strategies we're going to discuss do not pertain to options. If leverage is desired on a short-term basis, it can be achieved by holding a leveraged ETF, such as the ProShares Ultra Gold (UGL) ETF, which holds futures contracts on the shareholder's behalf. It aims to replicate 2X the daily movement of gold. If leverage is desired on a medium- to long-term basis, it can be achieved by investing in gold mining stocks.

The forex market is notorious for allowing traders to assume highly-leveraged positions. The fluctuation in most currency pairs is so small that the only way to build wealth quickly (or more likely, lose wealth quickly) is with leverage. The amount of leverage you can apply will vary by dealer, but most forex platforms enable account holders to control $100 worth of currency for every $1 they invest. Others might allow account holders to control $500 worth of currency for just a dollar. Most platforms also enable account holders to take leveraged positions in gold. Gold is technically money, so it makes sense that a forex broker would provide exposure. My advice is to stay away from these platforms, not just for gold, but for forex trading in general. The leverage offered by these brokers isn't safe. On top of that, the industry suffers from a lack of regulation. I don't understand why so many people get involved in trading forex, but I do understand why so many walk away. The stock market, for example, is like a casino where the odds are stacked in favor of the long-term investor. If the investor hedges their position with a modest gold allocation, the odds improve. When it comes to trading gold and foreign currencies through an online forex broker, the odds are undeniably stacked in the broker's favor.

These are high level examples of derivatives, their use, and their dangers. Obviously, gold isn't the only asset class for which derivatives are available. While I've provided simple examples of how the gold buyer can benefit from selling call options and the gold holder can benefit from buying protective puts, the use of derivatives can be extremely complicated. These instruments are typically utilized by experienced hedge fund managers and skilled investors who have dedicated countless hours (and dollars) to perfecting the craft. Derivatives are also utilized by foolish traders who have yet to lose large sums of money (but many of them eventually will).

A thorough discussion of derivatives is beyond the scope of *The Art and Science of Investing in Gold.* It's important to understand that gold investments exist in this form, that there are simple uses of derivatives that can provide simple benefits, and that aside from these uses, most derivatives lend themselves to speculation and high risk. A true gold buff might think an ETF that holds gold in trust is a risky investment, but it pales in comparison to the risk of investing in gold via exotic derivatives.

Scams

The gold investor is susceptible to scams. As we've seen, gold can be bought and sold in a variety of forms, and gold doesn't always trade on a regulated exchange. Like the forex market, the market for gold is global. With the exception of forex trading, there are more scams in gold than any other asset class.

While it's true that stock investors can fall victim to the likes of Bernie Madoff, the fact that stocks trade on a regulated exchange provides greater assurance that you're actually getting the stock that you paid for. This doesn't prevent one of your holdings from turning into the next Enron, but those who did invest in Enron stock through an established exchange at least received the stock that they paid for. This isn't always the case with gold. A fundamental difference between stocks and gold when it comes to scams is that it's easier for the little guy to pull scams in the gold market. They don't have to orchestrate an elaborate Ponzi scheme. Gold can be counterfeited. Online dealers don't necessarily have the gold that they advertise. Some of them are drop shippers who don't acquire gold until they receive an order from the customer. Others have no intention of making delivery.

I won't name the company, but the most interesting gold scam that I've heard about was pulled on a team of highly educated stock analysts. One of the analysts was a gold investor and had recently ordered gold from a bullion dealer with whom he had not previously done business. The bullion dealer bent over backwards for him. Not only did he supply investment grade bullion, but he personally delivered the bullion to the stock analyst's office. The other analysts witnessed the delivery and were immediately jealous. They wanted bullion too. Unlike their stocks, they wanted to be able to hold it and admire it, just as their colleague did. So the bullion dealer took their orders, collected his payment in advance, and then was never seen nor heard from again. The scam worked because the bullion dealer established clout. The other analysts saw him do business with a colleague who they trusted. This trust was then extended to the bullion dealer. It can happen to the best of us. That's why we need to be discerning in our actions. The truth is, most scams are easy to avoid. Let's have a look at what else we're up against.

In 2016, Northwest Territorial Mint filed for bankruptcy protection, while $50 M worth of gold bullion orders were never delivered. The owner of Northwest Territorial Mint claims that the solvency of his company deteriorated after he lost a defamation of character lawsuit. He'd started a website where he alleged that a former landlord had engaged in tactics that resembled the actions of Bernie Madoff. Even before the lawsuit, customers report having waited as long as 10 weeks for their gold to be delivered, which begs the question if the owner of Northwest Territorial Mint wasn't the one pulling Madoff-like tactics.

In 2018, a precious metals dealer was handed a $15.7 M civil monetary penalty for misappropriating investor funds. Basically, he sold them rights to gold that didn't exist.

In late 2019, the owner of Bullion Direct Inc. was convicted of two counts of wire fraud and one count of engaging in monetary transactions with criminally derived property. The fraud is estimated to have cost investors $16 M in capital.

Online dealers who sell below the spot price are hosting a scam. The only way they can legitimately make money is to charge a premium, so steer clear of those who don't. Don't chase the lowest price. It's never worth it. At the same time, don't overpay. Given that the spot price is public information, buying just above market value shouldn't be difficult.

A long wait time is another red flag. There's no reason why your bullion should take more than a week to arrive. If it takes longer, it means the dealer is selling bullion that he doesn't have yet. It could mean that he has no intention of delivering. He could be working under a different name and out of a different office the following week. Or maybe he does intend to deliver. If he's drop shipping, it means he orders his inventory after the customer places an order. It's not illegal, but it creates risk. If solvency issues arise, outstanding orders will go unfulfilled.

It's not possible to completely eliminate the risk of falling victim to a scam. This applies not just to investments, but to any type of purchase. When it comes to investing in gold, there are measures that can be taken to reduce your exposure to fraud.

Always buy through a reputable dealer. Read customer reviews. Visit their location. Ask to read their buyback policy. If they sell online, look for reviews on unrelated sites. Ask your stock broker if they can recommend a dealer. Ask yourself if the price they are selling at makes sense, both for you as an investor and for them as a profit-driven dealer. Then, if they seem trustworthy, start with a small purchase. You might even want to sell some of it back before you buy more, just to verify that they adhere to their buyback policy.

The reputation of a vaulting service is easy to verify online. Again, look for reviews on unrelated sites. Visit chat rooms and message boards where gold investors interact. Stay in the chat room and on the message board long enough to get a feel for who's genuine and who's there just to advertise. Talk to people who have used the same service. You can again check with your stock broker, but with vaulting services, it might be more difficult to get a recommendation, especially for vaults located in foreign countries. Though it never hurts to ask.

Avoid dealers that don't have a long history. This is an area where you need to separate your emotions from your investment decisions. A lot of people take satisfaction in supporting up-and-coming businesses. That's great if you're talking about a new mom and pop restaurant, a local grocery store, or if one of your friends thinks he can brew a better cup of coffee than Starbucks. By all means, support them with your patronage. Just remember that bullion is different. If a dealer goes under, it means the buyback policy is void. If you bought from an online dealer, it means your order might never arrive. My goal isn't to work against the aspiring bullion dealer, but to encourage investors to make smart decisions.

Buy smaller bars. We already discussed the pros and cons. You pay a higher premium per ounce, but you're able to sell just a portion of your holdings at a time. On top of that, small bars are less likely to be counterfeited. Counterfeiters are greedy and they don't waste their time nickel-and-diming with small increments of gold. If you only buy small, it's less likely that counterfeit gold will make its way into your possession. If it does, hopefully it's just a few small bars, as opposed to that one great big bar you might otherwise have bought.

Ironically, the gold ETF protects us against scams, even though it exposes us to the very same risk that gold is supposed to protect us against, that being the risk of a financial system collapse. When you buy shares in the SPDR Gold Shares (GLD) ETF or the iShares Gold Trust (IAU) ETF, you should have confidence that HSBC and JP Morgan, respectively, are holding the required amounts of gold in trust. This should alleviate concerns of being sold counterfeit gold, that the gold you ordered might never arrive, or of a buyback policy not being honored. The shares of these ETFs trade on a regulated exchange, fluctuate in accordance to the spot price, and are highly liquid. This is a great way to increase your exposure to gold as you decrease your exposure to scams. But be aware, if we ever return to a 2007-2008-like catastrophe, the banks aren't bailed out, and the institution that holds your gold in trust becomes insolvent, a lengthy and expensive proceeding that involves many highly-compensated attorneys could ensue. Should this happen, the salvage value of your shares is going to be impaired.

Don't put all of your eggs in one basket

A smart investor understands the advantages (and disadvantages) of diversification. It offers protection through all stages of the economic cycle, but at certain stages, it holds us back. While it would be foolish to forgo diversification completely, there are identifiable stages in the economic cycle when overweighting in favor of gold makes sense. Even during these stages, we don't want our baskets filled with nothing but golden eggs. Diversification should be maintained at all times. Markets are constantly evolving and they have the potential to behave in ways that they haven't previously behaved. There are times when the "predictable" stage of the market cycle is your best friend, and times when your best friend behaves in such a way as to cause embarrassment.

We don't just want to diversify in terms of the assets we hold, but also in terms of how we hold them. Gold is gold, but as we now know, the different ways to invest in gold present a diverging mix of advantages and disadvantages. ETFs are great for convenience and ease of execution. Most investors prefer ETFs in terms of portfolio rebalancing and timing short-term movements. That doesn't mean gold can't be held concurrently via other methods. A modest stack of gold coins in your house might come in handy if you have an urgent need for liquidity and the banks aren't open. Bullion held by a vaulting service protects you from a bank holiday while keeping burglars like

Bill Mason out of your house. Diversifying across different asset classes is crucial. Diversifying how we invest in gold provides added benefit. Go ahead and use an ETF for its convenience. Bury a few bars in your back yard. Stash a few coins under your mattress. Use a vaulting service you trust. And invest in lots and lots of other assets. Then, when fear is on the horizon and high inflation seems imminent, reduce your exposure to some of those other assets as you increase your exposure to gold. We'll discuss how to do that in Chapter 8.

Chapter 5: Pricing

Don't worry, we're about to talk strategy. That's why you're reading this, right? To form a strategy. We'll get there. But first, it's important to have a firm grasp on what drives the price of gold. I've already alluded to a number of factors. Supply and demand come into play, as do the emotions of fear and greed. Unlike the stock market, which is propelled higher and higher as greed takes over, fear is what drives the price of gold. As a result, stocks and gold have a tendency to move in opposite directions. This isn't always the case, but you'll find very observable instances when these asset classes behave like complete opposites. We're going to take advantage of that with our strategy.

When greed is rampant, stocks go up and gold goes down. When the smart money gets nervous with the stock market, they gradually take their money back. Some will sit on cash, others will invest in gold. When this trend begins, stocks and gold will then move higher in tandem, but this correlation is going to deteriorate as more and more investors decrease their stock exposure in favor of gold. From there, the inflation that everyone is betting on either pans out or it doesn't. That stock market crash that everyone is predicting either happens or it doesn't. The fear that drove investors into gold either pays off or it's alleviated. Perhaps it's just postponed. Whatever the case, trends form, and these trends have an observable impact on the spot price of gold. The emotions of fear and greed can bat the price around like a tennis ball.

To simply state that fear moves the price of gold higher is an oversimplification. Typically, the initial movement is the result of fear, and what keeps the price moving higher is an increase in the real rate of inflation. Gold is a precious metal that's limited in supply, earns no income, pays no dividends, and is the oldest form of money that we know. It's an accepted store of value. That's why it responds to changes in the real rate of inflation.

The spurts in the economic cycle during which fear prevails are fewer and shorter than the periods during which greed prevails. For this reason, the opportunities to make money with gold—not just hedge our bets, but make real money—are fewer than with assets that advance when the herd is greedy.

The spot price of gold is tracked in U.S. dollars, not just in the United States, but globally. This keeps the price uniform across regions. Countries are then at liberty to translate the spot price to their local currency, but by doing so, it causes currency fluctuations. At the time of writing, an ounce of gold is priced at $1,900 USD.

Gold is an interesting asset because it can't be evaluated the same way as other securities. Stocks, bonds, and real estate are all very different, but they can all be analyzed according to their intrinsic value. Each asset is expected to produce a stream of income in the future. We wouldn't buy them if they didn't. Publicly traded companies report earnings and pay dividends. Bonds pay interest (for most bonds, the amount that's going to be paid is known at the time of purchase). Real estate earns rent and tax deductions. To determine what any of these assets are worth, we take the expected future cash flows, discount them back to their present value, and then sum the total. If you took Finance 101 in college, the present value calculation is one of the first things they taught you. If you're scratching your head at the concept, don't worry, there are plenty of YouTube videos that can clarify the concept with a few brief examples—*isn't technology wonderful!*

Intrinsic value is important because it helps investors determine if an investment is selling at a reasonable price. If an asset is priced below its intrinsic value, it's viewed as a potential buy. If it's priced above its intrinsic value, it might be time to sell. In order to make the right buy and sell decisions, the investor needs to come up with an intrinsic value that's relatively accurate. Their prediction of future cash flows needs to be reasonable, as does their prediction of the discount factor, which is essentially a prediction of the future rate of inflation. Needless to say, a lot of these predictions are wrong, and a lot of the buying and selling that happens in the market is the result of other factors. But that doesn't stop the herd from trying.

There are plenty of investors who base their strategy on trying to identify undervalued securities. Gold might be viewed as undervalued when the price has been beaten down. This happens when there are more sellers than buyers, and certain buyers will step up to the plate to grab some gold at what they perceive to be a discount. Whether or not this strategy provides a decent return depends on many factors. We know that gold set a new high in 1980 at $850 per ounce, but then fell into bear territory and didn't return to this level until 2006. We also know that gold provided a 1300% return between 1971 and 1980. This precious metal certainly has its ups and downs, but without a readily determined intrinsic value, it's difficult to determine if gold is priced at a discount or if it's simply been beaten down to a price that's reasonable.

Gold is rarely the asset of choice for value investors. Expressing gold's intrinsic value in dollar terms is like trying to row a boat without a paddle. We have to put the concept of intrinsic value on the back-burner and focus on how the emotions of fear and greed impact the price of gold. The forces that move gold are similar to the forces that move the stock market. With stocks, it's the buying and selling of institutional investors that moves the market. With gold, it's mostly the buying and selling of central banks and the International Monetary Fund. In either market, the individual investor is just along for the ride. We can buy and sell gold at the prevailing price, but our actions don't move markets unless we act in unison. In other words, a herd has to form in order for individual investors to have an impact. Even when we account for the fact that the gold market is comparatively smaller than the stock, bond, and real estate markets, it still requires herd mentality for individual investors to move the market.

In 2019, the World Gold Council estimated that a total of 190,000 metric tons of gold have been mined to date. Assuming a spot price of $1,900, this equates to almost $11.5 trillion in value. It sounds like a lot, but in the U.S. alone, the stock, bond, and real estate markets are each larger than the global market for gold. The U.S. stock market is currently valued at $30 trillion, which is almost three times the value of all the gold in circulation. The bond market is valued at almost $40 trillion, with U.S. Treasuries representing $14 trillion of the total. The commercial real estate market is estimated to be worth somewhere between $14 and $17 trillion, and the housing market weighs in at a whopping $33 trillion.

Gold and real estate are both fixed in quantity. Even though we continue to mine for gold, the total supply of gold, including both gold in circulation and gold that is still beneath the earth, is fixed. Similarly, we can construct new buildings, but the land that we build on is fixed. Both of these markets are influenced by scarcity. This notion of scarcity doesn't apply to the stock and bond markets. There's no limit to the number of companies that can go public, just as there's no limit to the amount of debt that can be issued. Scarcity, on the other hand, is the largest factor in determining the price of gold.

Of the 190,000 tons of gold in circulation, 2/3 was mined after 1950. As investors, we have access to the largest gold market that the world has ever seen. We're also operating in a world that's highly connected. We now know that gold is selling at the same price in Russia, Switzerland, Japan, and even the Cayman Islands. When central banks become bullish on gold, their propensity to move the market is greater than the propensity of institutional investors to move the stock market. Again, scarcity is at the forefront. It doesn't take as much buying to send the price higher. This explains why sudden and unexpected increases in the price can be so fierce. It also explains why gold derivatives are so dangerous (there's simply not enough gold to support all of the options contracts in circulation).

Now, consider the fact that central banks all around the globe stockpile gold. It's not just the common man who gets scared when the economy starts to overheat. Governments get scared, too. Their reaction is the same as ours—*they buy gold!* But in many ways, their reaction is not as savvy as yours will be once you're done with this book. Most central banks aren't strategic in how they buy gold. It's strictly a fear mechanism. Many central banks end up buying when the price is high (out of fear), only to sell when the price is low (after the fear subsides).

Central banks don't just buy gold. They buy a lot of assets and they buy them for many different reasons. They also have the ability to print money in order to buy these assets (something you and I would be arrested for). So we combine inflation with the ability of major central banks to move markets, and what we see is that an asset like gold, which serves as a hedge against inflation, is hit with a two-pronged effect: (1) printing currency so that central banks can buy assets leads to inflation, and (2) the act of central banks investing in gold increases demand. With the stock market, the reaction is spread out. Some sectors of the stock market benefit from inflation, while others do worse. Gold is gold. When central banks print money, we can expect a subsequent increase in the spot price of gold. When central banks buy gold, the demand moves the market higher.

The impact that scarcity has on gold is important, but scarcity is solely a measure of supply; it doesn't create demand. There's a demand for gold because it's extremely malleable, easy to reshape and transform, and it doesn't corrode or rust. This is important for jewelry, but also important for money. Gold is a symbol of wealth due to both appearance and the fact that it can't be destroyed. That's why it's the oldest money that we have. Dollar bills are destroyed all the time. It's just paper. But gold persists. There are plenty of metals that are rarer than gold but sell for less because they don't hold these properties. There's less demand.

Another factor influencing the price of gold is the fact that it's difficult to manipulate. A company can easily manipulate their earnings report with accounting trickery. Some of this trickery is perfectly legal as long as it's disclosed in a footnote. Other trickery, not so much. That's the great thing about gold. It's fixed in quantity and it has no earnings. It can be counterfeited, but it can't be manipulated. That's why gold is such a powerful hedge against inflation. There's a limited supply in the world. At certain stages in the economic cycle, demand is incredibly strong.

Chapter 6: The Art and Science of Strategy

It can be argued that all facets of investing lend themselves to both art and science. This includes investing in stocks, bonds, real estate, non-traditional asset classes like fine art and wine, and especially gold. How much of a given approach is comprised of art and how much is comprised of science depends on how actively one manages the investment. Indexing, for example, is mostly science. You gain exposure to an entire market with a single instrument and then stay put as the market appreciates in value. This is a widely accepted science with relatively predictable long-term results. Modern portfolio theory is also a science. Investors determine their tolerance for risk and then allocate their funds to different asset classes according to their tolerance. From there, the markets move. Different asset classes exhibit a wide range of performance. Some assets move in the same direction but at their own pace, while others do the exact opposite. Then everything changes. Asset classes that were once aligned break their correlation and move against each other. Some asset classes advance as others decline. Some move sideways. The asset allocator increases his wealth by rebalancing the portfolio as each asset class works through its respective cycle. It's all very scientific. The weight of each asset class can be measured. The frequency with which one rebalances their portfolio is predetermined. The long-term average return provided by each asset class is relatively predictable. One does not need to be an artist in order to reap the rewards; they simply need to acquire a basic understanding of modern portfolio theory. From there, it's all very mathematical. Rebalance. Rebalance. Rebalance. Lower your tolerance for risk as you age. Rebalance. Rebalance. Rebalance.

When gold is used as a hedge, it's a science. Conventional wisdom suggests an allocation between 5% and 10%. When gold is used as more than a hedge and becomes the driving factor of wealth accumulation, it becomes an art. A hedge can be held through every stage of the economic cycle, where an asset that's relied upon to build wealth will only outperform during specific stages of the cycle.

It should be noted that the art and science of investing are not mutually exclusive. Both can be performed simultaneously. It's nearly impossible to build a retirement without making investments. I firmly believe that everyone should practice the science of investing. If, in addition to building a stable retirement by investing in index funds and following modern portfolio theory, you also want investments that you actively manage, it's best to do so with separate funds. When one pursues the art of investing, I tend to think of it as a side bet. The art should not replace the science, but be performed in addition to the science. If you're invested in a 401(k) or have other means of saving for retirement, that's where the science takes place. Don't disturb it. When you think gold is on the brink of a new bull run, leave the science alone. There's a reason why your asset classes are allocated the way they are. Let your holdings work through their cycles. Let modern portfolio theory work its magic. Rebalance. Rebalance. Rebalance.

Side bets should be made with discretionary income that you can afford to lose. Naturally, you don't want to lose the money, but the psychology of market timing changes when your standard of living isn't on the line. It would be foolish to throw 60% of your 401(k) at gold because you think now is the time to buy. If you do and gold doesn't go up, you're going to lose sleep. The lower gold goes, the more nervous you'll become. Eventually, you'll regret the decision and pull out. After that, anything can happen. Maybe the gold bull will come charging through as soon as you close your position. This type of mistake doesn't happen with a properly diversified portfolio, and it's less likely to happen when making a side bet with your discretionary income.

Getting in and out of your investments at lucrative points in the economic cycle is an art. By definition, not everyone is going to master it. For those who try, gold lends itself to this art because of its scarcity. The luxury of dollar cost averaging as you wait for wealth to accumulate is reserved for the stock investor. The opportunity to earn large returns over short periods of time belongs to the gold investor. Stocks can also be timed, but to truly outperform the market, one must select the right stock at the right time, where the gold investor is only tasked with selecting the right time.

A bull run in gold has the propensity to provide larger returns than a bull run in stocks, but the period of time during which the gold bull rages tends to be much shorter. This creates both advantages and disadvantages. The potential reward is higher, as is the level of skill required to earn the reward. In the stock market, slow and steady gains are easily captured through a mechanism known as luck. Between 2009 and 2020, investors were lucky. It didn't take skill. All you had to do was make an investment.

With the advent of the index fund, investors are able to build wealth on the stock market without truly understanding how the market functions. This might sound like a cynical statement, but it's not. The ability to build wealth without becoming an expert in stocks is empowering. Employees are now responsible for their own retirements and the 401(k) is the vehicle that facilitates this responsibility. From there, the index fund empowers them. We all get to share in the prosperity of the stock market. Our daily tasks may revolve around improving our employer's position in a competitive market, but through the index fund, we prosper simultaneously from the sum of everyone's contribution.

Gold is different. The market doesn't move higher as a result of hard work and innovation, it moves higher when certain pillars of our financial structure weaken. Gold might serve as a lucrative hedge for the 401(k) investor, but it shouldn't be given the blind reliance that the majority of the workforce gives to the stock market.

Gold is a unique investment for three reasons. First, it has an inverse relationship to the dollar. The Federal Reserve can instruct the Treasury to print as many dollars as it wants, while the gold supply remains relatively constant.

The second reason is that gold can't go bankrupt. The stock investor can diversify away the risk of a specific company filing for bankruptcy by investing in many companies. Once this is done, the stock investor is tasked with diversifying away the risk of the entire stock market taking a hit. Gold aids in this endeavor.

Gold tends to move against equities. When stocks and real estate are doing well, gold is often in the dumps. When equities take a turn for the worst, gold is likely to rally. With stocks, the average bull market outlasts the average bear market by an average of three years. Gold, on the other hand, can easily spend more time in bear territory than it spends in bull territory. From an economic standpoint, a prolonged bull market in gold is a cause for concern—*but it does happen.*

This depiction of gold moving against equities is a bit of an oversimplification. There are times when gold moves in tandem with stocks and times when it moves against stocks. It spends enough time moving against stocks that the asset classes aren't viewed as being positively correlated. This is the third reason why gold is a unique investment.

During the 2007-2008 financial crisis, when stocks and real estate tanked, gold initially moved in the same direction before it sharply changed course and shot through the roof. It took almost ten years for stocks to catch up and then take the lead. At the time of writing, real estate still hasn't caught up. Those who used gold as a hedge and rebalanced their portfolio throughout the recovery would have systematically sold shares of their gold ETF while picking up stocks and real estate at huge discounts. As stocks and real estate recovered, they'd have then done just the opposite, selling equities to reinvest in gold and putting themselves in a great position for the coronavirus crash of 2020. In addition to this, if you held a side bet in gold, you had the potential to make even more money. It all depends on when you enter and exit the market. Each investor has their own approach. The one thing each successful approach has in common is that it relies on at least one economic indicator.

Chapter 7: The Art of Economic Indicators

Gold shines at specific stages in the economic cycle. The better we get at identifying the stages, the better we understand the risk, reward, and potential consequences of investing in gold. We rely on economic indicators in order to make projections on where the spot price of gold is headed, but it's rare for all of the indicators to tell us the same thing at the same time. It would be great if they all chimed simultaneously, but if we wait for this to happen, we'll miss some really good entry points and end up buying at the top. Instead, we want to keep our eye on a handful of the more telling economic indicators, and then make our move when we start to encounter convincing signals. A leading indicator might suggest that it's time to dip our toes in the water, while a lagging indicator might tell us that it's time to average up on our holding.

We want the same thing from each indicator that we follow—*a buy signal!* But each indicator is a little different. Some indicators are cyclical in nature and are only relevant at certain stages of the cycle. Others are more abstract, like fear. Yes, we're going to use fear as an economic indicator. We're also going to look at the CBOE Volatility Index, stock market crashes, signals from famous investors, the actions of central banks, Gross Domestic Product (GDP), inflation, deflation, quantitative easing, interest rates, and hyperinflation. It sounds like a lot, and it is. Gold can be a very complex asset. My advice is to become familiar with the economic indicators that foretell when a bull is coming, but again, don't expect all them to chime simultaneously. It's never that easy. It's a process of using multiple indicators to survey the environment and then making your move when one or two compelling signals start to flash.

If you read *Beating The Market*, then you already know how I apply economic indicators. You also know that I take them with a grain of salt. That's because markets aren't static, but constantly evolving. This is especially true of the stock market.

The very nature of what the stock market is prevents it from doing something exactly as it did before. Product lines change. Consumer preferences change. The services available continue to broaden. With innovation, the amount of value that publicly traded companies create is limitless. That's part of why stocks keep trading at higher prices. They become more expensive not just due to inflation, but by providing innovative products and services that create value. Gold can't do this. As we know, gold is gold, just like coffee is coffee. The stock market and the gold market are both cyclical, but the fact that gold is always gold means there won't be any outliers that go higher while the rest of the market tanks. When gold falls into bear territory, all gold falls into bear territory. There's no Amazon Inc (AMZN) equivalent that keeps going higher. As a result, economic indicators provide greater predictive value for gold than they do for stocks. We know exactly how gold is going to react to high inflation. I still take my economic indicators with a grain of salt, but when it comes to gold, the grains are much smaller.

Fear

We're going to cover 13 different economic indicators, but when you get down to it, each of these indicators is just an extension of the single most important driving factor behind the price of gold—*fear!*

Fear is the indicator that we care about the most. When people get scared—of recessions, job losses, bank holidays, excessive quantitative easing, hyperinflation, financial Armageddon, etc—the price of gold goes up. The deeper the fear, the higher the appreciation. It's human nature to mitigate fear, not just by purchasing gold, but by enacting fiscal policy aimed at combating all of the things that send gold higher. Policy makers are constantly working to keep the stock market and their fiscal currency healthy, often at the expense of gold. For this reason, prolonged bull runs in gold are less common, but not unheard of. If you refer back to the charts in Chapter 2, you'll notice that the quick yet fierce bull run from 1979 to 1980 was followed by a 26-year dry spell. In 1980, gold stood at $590 per ounce. It fell into bear territory and didn't return to this level until 2006. The bull run that brought gold back into favor started in 2000 when gold was priced at only $270. It lasted for 12 years. This is unusual for gold, because 12-year bull runs don't typically happen without 12 years of fear. But that's exactly what we had. It started with 9/11, followed by the dot-com bust, and it didn't end until after the subprime mortgage crisis.

Bull markets always lead to bear markets. It doesn't matter what asset class we're looking at; markets move in cycles. Gold is no exception. When fear leads to rapid gains, it's likely that a bubble will form . . . *and then burst*. It's not much different from what we see time and again in the stock market, except gold bubbles have the potential to form much faster, depending on the severity of the fear.

As we move through the following economic indicators, keep in mind that each indicator only has predictive value if it corresponds with fear. Inflation alone doesn't push the price of gold higher. If the U.S., Europe, and China all experience healthy levels of inflation without any corresponding fear, gold could just as easily decline in value. But when inflation accelerates beyond healthy levels, it will be accompanied by fear, and the price of gold is going to rise.

Gold as an Economic Indicator

Sometimes an asset class is also an economic indicator. The stock market, for example, isn't merely a mechanism for investing in publicly traded companies, but is also an economic indicator. It's known as a leading indicator because people invest based on their perceived outlook of the future. When the stock market is overpriced and investors continue to buy more and push it higher, it's because their future outlook is bullish. When stocks are dirt cheap and only the smart money is willing to touch them, it's because most of the other investors have a bearish outlook.

Gold also serves as an economic indicator. It tells us when fear is present. When the demand for gold goes up, we know that fear drove it up. This isn't a guarantee that the fear will persist, but it tells us that fear is present nonetheless. From there, we ask questions. Are individual investors buying? Are the central banks buying? Did Warren Buffet or George Soros just buy a bunch of gold in spite of the fact that they're notorious gold bears? The answers to these questions tell volumes about the level of fear that we're dealing with.

When fear isn't present, we only want to hold gold as a portfolio hedge. In the stock market, it's common to buy more simply because the market has been beaten down. We should have confidence that the stock market will recover and then go on to set new highs. Gold is a little different. If we buy when it's down—at a time when fear is scarce and everyone's happy—we could spend 26 years waiting for the next gold bull to come charging through. That's not a game I care to play. Gold is an asset class where contrarians and value investors are seldom rewarded. We want to follow the herd, not for so long that we fall off the same cliff that they're eventually going to fall from, but instead want to join the herd when the fear is young and still has room left to run.

At the time of writing, we're in an environment plagued with concerns of a prolonged recession, trade war with China, and low interest rates combined with the printing of more fiat currency, all while the central banks of India, China, and Russia are stockpiling gold. Gold has gone up and we expect it to continue going up. This isn't an ideal economic landscape, but it's an ideal environment for investing in gold. The gold investor has to wait patiently to encounter such an environment, and will in all likelihood be invested in other asset classes as they wait. As the pieces described above fall into place, the gold investor will reduce exposure to other holdings as they increase their exposure to gold. The length of this position is contingent on either the length of the recession or the duration of time over which recessionary concerns persist. A top will eventually form and, like with any other asset class, calling the top is next to impossible. Instead of striving to achieve the impossible endeavor of getting in at the bottom and out at the top, the successful gold investor will gradually increase their exposure as the economic outlook worsens, and then gradually reduce their exposure as gains materialize. In other words, they move in shifts. Knowing when to keep buying and when to start selling is what makes this an art. It pays to diversify across a variety of asset classes at all points in the cycle, but we also want to diversify across time. When fear sets in and gold advances, we buy. Should gold continue to advance, we average up and buy more. We continue in shifts as the central banks continue to increase their exposure. Our goal is to get out before the fear subsides. Those who use gold as a portfolio hedge, say 5% to 10% of their holdings, will continue to hold the asset class once the economy improves, while those who strive to increase their gains even more by placing a side bet in gold are tasked with getting out before it's too late.

CBOE Volatility Index (VIX)

Gold isn't the only indicator that tells us when fear is present. The Chicago Board Options Exchange (also called the VIX or the "Fear Index") is an index that measures volatility over the next 30 days based on price inputs of the S&P 500 index options. An increase in the price of stock options is an indication of volatility. The likelihood that an option will expire in the money (or above zero) increases as volatility increases. As a result, higher options prices correspond with higher volatility, which in turn is an indicator of fear. Investors often dump stocks and revert to cash when the VIX rises. The best time to get back in on stocks is right when the VIX peaks. It's next to impossible to call the peak, but savvy investors will learn to recognize a peak after it forms and then get back in on stocks as the VIX trends lower. The gold investor, on the other hand, will do just the opposite. When the VIX is rising we want to hold gold, and after it peaks we want to dump gold.

Here's a chart of the VIX from 2004 through 2019. Each of the spikes corresponds with an opportunity to earn large short-term gains in gold. From late 2008 through late 2011, there was also ample opportunity to earn even larger long-term returns, but the VIX isn't an indicator for long-term gold investments. We'll get to those shortly. For now, be aware that a spike in the VIX is likely to correspond with a lucrative short-term buy-in opportunity for gold.

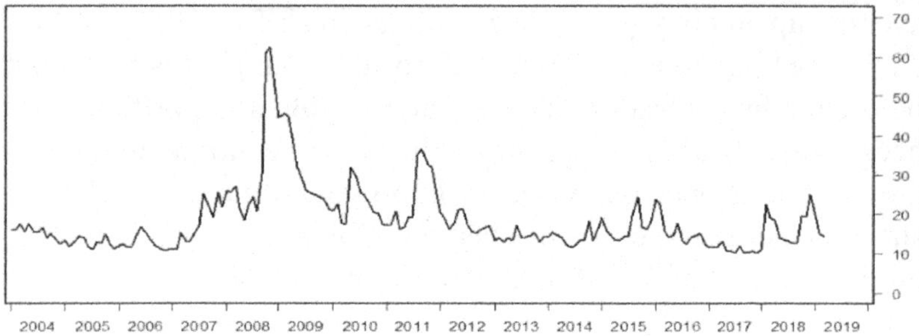

Stock Market Crash

A trusted hedge should work its magic when the market that we're hedging against crashes. That's why we hedge with gold, because it's supposed to provide strong returns when the stock market gets beaten down. But how often do we really see a crash coming? We might recognize that the stock market looks expensive. Similarly, we might recognize that it keeps getting more expensive as more years pass. Eventually it's going to crash, it's just that we don't know when. And when it does crash, if we haven't already placed a side bet in gold, then it's too late, right? *The answer might surprise you.*

Yes, gold provides protection against a stock market crash, but as we discussed in Chapter 2, there's often a lag between when the stock market crashes and when gold really takes off. For this reason, a stock market crash serves as an economic indicator. It provides predictive value on the direction of gold. Don't make the mistake of thinking that a stock market crash means it's too late to get in on gold. In all likelihood, the crash will pull gold down with it, albeit temporarily, and this creates an amazing buy-in opportunity for gold (and stocks, too).

Investors (as a whole) don't behave rationally leading up to and during a stock market crash. If they did behave rationally there wouldn't be bubbles and crashes. We'd all do an adequate job of calculating the intrinsic value of each and every security, and they would all sell for a price that's very close to said intrinsic value. For prolonged stages of the stock market cycle, this is what happens; the market behaves efficiently. But greed eventually takes over, which leads to bubbles, and the market eventually crashes, which coincides with fear. The deeper the crash, the greater the chance that fear will persist.

A stock market crash is defined as a sudden and dramatic decline in stock prices across a major cross-section of the stock market, resulting in significant loss of paper wealth. Crashes are driven not only by economic factors, but also by panic selling. It's important to highlight that only "paper wealth" is lost. The crash wreaks havoc on our portfolios, but wealth hasn't actually been destroyed. There are still the same number of dollars in circulation before the crash as immediately after the crash. More fiat currency is likely to be printed, but it hasn't happened yet. What really happens during a stock market crash is that wealth is transferred. The balance of our stock holdings goes down while the balance of our gold holdings goes up. The crash that causes this is of course unexpected. It creates confusion for stock investors, but also provides predictive value to gold investors. Think of it as a smoke screen. Those who don't understand how markets function are trapped in a fog, while the savvy investor analyzes the environment in order to take a winning position.

When the stock market crashes it tends to take other asset classes down with it. This frustrates a lot of investors because they thought gold was going to protect them from the crash—*be patient, it will!* Give gold a week or so to recover. When stocks tank, there's panic selling and a need for liquidity. Investors that use leverage are going to receive margin calls, and this forces them to liquidate unrelated assets in order to cover their margin calls. So they sell some of their gold. Or their broker liquidates holdings in a gold ETF on their behalf. Other investors become so overwhelmed with fear that they make decisions based on emotion rather than reason. This behavior spills over into other markets. The deeper the crash, the deeper the drag across unrelated markets, even those that are defensive in nature. The stock market will behave irrationally as it struggles to find direction. It can wallow in the doldrums for as long as it pleases. It might recover quickly. It might not. Investors don't know what their stocks are really worth and the longer it takes the market to stabilize, the better the buy-in opportunity for defensive markets that were prematurely dragged down amongst the panic selling. This is a rare situation where the value investor can definitively say that gold is priced at a discount. They don't want stocks until they see signs of a bottom forming. Instead, they want gold. Precious metals are going to recover before stocks, and in all likelihood provide huge returns before the stock market has a chance to catch up.

Look how gold behaved during the 2007-2008 financial crisis. Going into the crisis, it wasn't a secret that the economy was overheated (we simply didn't understand the extent to which it was going to collapse). Investors were already moving into gold when the stock market started showing signs of weakness. When what initially looked like a correction for stocks turned into a crash, gold took a preemptive hit. Then it rebounded and shot through the roof. The stock market took longer to find its bottom. It eventually recovered and moved higher, but failed to keep pace with gold.

A housing crisis of this magnitude should rightfully force investors to question the value of their equity holdings. An asset like gold is different. There's limited quantity. Central banks stock pile it in case of emergencies. The probability of more dollars being printed in order to provide stimulus packages is exceptionally high. When gold takes a beating along with the stock market, it's not a sign that investors have been duped, but an indication that they should buy more.

We saw a similar phenomenon with the advent of the coronavirus pandemic. Leading into 2020, both gold and stocks were trending higher. Some investors were caught up in the euphoria of an overpriced stock market that insisted on becoming even more overpriced, while cautious investors were increasing their exposure to gold. Both asset classes spent greater than a year trending higher as they fought for the lead. They traded places on several occasions. But again, when the stock market crashed, defensive assets were pulled down with it. Panic selling set in. Margin calls erupted. There was both a sense of fear and a need for liquidity and it again spilled over into unrelated markets. Gold initially took a hit when it should have been playing defense. Then it recovered and continued to ascend higher.

While gold is in the lead at the time of writing, it's interesting that stocks bounced back so ferociously. Unlike the 2007-2008 financial crisis where the solvency of big banks put our entire economic infrastructure at risk, what we see here is a division between big business and small business. Savvy tech companies are thriving as the world shifts to a predominately remote work environment. Amazon is still dropping packages off on our doorsteps. Grocery stores have never experienced higher sales. But certain restaurants are suffering, barbershops have been boycotted, and no one wants to exercise at a public gym. The stock market is not the same as the economy and the schism between the two is growing wider. At the time of writing, the investor who bought the dip in stocks has fared better than the investor who bought the dip in gold. But investors who held gold before the crash and simply saw things through have outperformed investors who did the same with stocks.

When it comes to the science of investing in gold, the asset allocator is better off having experienced the crash than they would be if stocks simply trended higher at a reasonable pace. It doesn't matter what your rebalancing schedule is—some do it quarterly, others biennially, and some once a year—when the stock market tanks, it's time to rebalance. There's an added benefit to rebalancing off-cycle when markets make extreme moves. By doing so, you skim from the top of asset classes that have fared *much better* in order to reinvest in those that have been beaten down to *even deeper* discounts. This improves your position for the recovery.

When used as an indicator to time the gold market, a stock market crash is extremely reliable. It's not just the spillover effect that temporarily takes gold down with it, but also the economic changes that are likely to follow. Governments tend to adjust their fiscal policy in response to a crash. It doesn't happen overnight. Political systems tend to move slowly because they suffer from . . . well, they suffer from the very nature of politics. When they act quickly, it's a sign that the problem is more serious than we think. Whatever the pace, there's likely to be fiscal stimulus, quantitative easing, and subsidy programs, all while consumers are being very selective in how they spend their money. When more fiat currency is printed, high inflation will follow, and the bull market in gold will persist. To get the biggest bang for your buck, buy gold when it gets pulled down along with the stock market.

When bears become bulls

I'm not a big fan of listening to experts, at least not as far as my investments are concerned. In other facets of life, I wouldn't think or proceeding without the much-needed advice of an expert. When I need medical advice, I turn to an expert. When I need legal advice, I turn to an expert. But when it comes to making an investment decision, I don't want the "experts" anywhere near my portfolio. We live in a world where most actively managed mutual funds lag the index they're designed to beat. Most stock analysts and financial journalists care more about their employer's relationship with fund companies than they do with the best interest of the average investor. Most publications won't downgrade a stock if a mutual fund that advertises in the publication is invested in the stock. The journalists might even recommend the stock even if they wouldn't buy it themselves. That's just the way the world works. The best investment strategies are those that work despite what the "experts" are saying. A successful investor is one who can recognize a good investment without even paying attention to the analysts.

Gold, as I keep saying, is different. It's a store of value that, for the most part, doesn't even have to compete with other precious metals. It doesn't matter what the analysts say about gold. When investors add precious metals to their portfolio, they add gold. Some investors never buy gold. Or they think they'll never buy gold, but when the economic outlook becomes bleak and a bullish trend in gold starts to form, they might have a change of mind. One of the strongest buy signals is when a famous gold bear turns bullish.

As discussed in Chapter 3, George Soros is a notorious gold bear. In 2017, he caved and decided to take a bullish position in gold. Investors who bought gold simply because they noticed the change of sentiment did quite well. Warren Buffet is also an outspoken gold bear, but in 2020, he made a large investment in a gold mining stock, and the trend that followed was bullish. Kevin O'Leary likes to maintain a 5% portfolio hedge with gold, but is extraordinarily bearish of gold miners. Should he ever change his mind and make an investment in a gold mining stock, that too should be taken as a bullish signal.

When a gold expert says to buy gold, they might be right. You should survey the environment and decide whether or not you agree with them. When a notorious gold bear buys gold, the probability that gold will continue in an upward trend is much stronger. The only reason to be on the sideline is if you know something they don't.

Central Banks

All investments appreciate for the same reason: demand exceeds supply. This is the most basic facet of investing. The more sophisticated investor won't just look at demand, but will want to know where the demand is coming from. A stock investor might want to know what Warren Buffett and George Soros are buying. They watch the smart money and they follow suit. Or they might want to know if insiders are buying. It's an extremely bullish sign when executives aren't content with the number of shares they've been awarded, but also want to buy more out of their own pocket. But gold isn't a company and there's no insider activity to follow. Instead, the gold investor turns his attention to the central banks. They, too, buy gold out of fear, and they do so in such large quantities that it moves markets.

Stocks and gold are fundamentally different, but the forces that move these markets are surprisingly similar. With stocks, it's the buying and selling of institutional investors that moves a stock higher or lower. Not only do institutional investors buy and sell in large quantities, they also like to play follow the leader. When a successful fund buys, other funds follow suit. When it sells, so do their followers. A hedge fund or mutual fund could also invest in gold, but the volume is typically much smaller than what is bought and sold by central banks. The behavior of central banks, however, mimics that of hedge funds and mutual funds; they have a tendency to watch other central banks and play follow the leader. When India, Australia, and the UK start buying gold in large quantities, other nations take note.

The gold investor could watch the volume of an ETF like the GLD to gauge the demand for gold, but it's important to understand that central banks aren't buying ETFs, they're buying bullion. The ETF is a convenient instrument for individual investors, but in order to observe trends in the demand for gold, they need to look outside of their ETF shell and take note of who's buying bullion. It's a bullish signal when the central banks start buying.

GDP and the debt-to-GDP ratio

We know the impact that a stock market crash has on gold. Now we're going to analyze gold in terms of GDP. We do this in addition to analyzing gold in relation to the stock market for one very important reason—the stock market is not the same as the economy. From an economic standpoint, the stock market is purely an economic indicator. It tells economists whether or not investors have confidence in the economy. It also tells economists how different sectors are performing.

Some investors make the mistake of thinking that the stock market cycle is synonymous with the economic cycle. It's an easy mistake to make because the cycles have a tendency to exhibit strong positive correlation. Stocks tend to sell at a premium when the economy performs well and then at a discount when the economic cycle bottoms. That is, until something breaks the correlation.

The coronavirus pandemic is a perfect example of the correlation breaking down. The U.S. entered into a recession in February of 2020. The stock market crashed in March of 2020. By May, the stock market had rebounded with strong indication of a V-shaped recovery, yet the economy was still in a recession. This divergence can be attributed to the fact that startups and small businesses, which account for 44% of economic activity, were suffering, while certain big businesses prospered. The quarantine had an advantageous impact on stocks like Netflix, Inc (NFLX); Amazon, Inc (AMZN); Apple, Inc (AAPL); The Clorox Company (CLX); Domino's Pizza, Inc. (DPZ); and Zoom Video Communications, Inc. (ZM). The large cap indexes bounced back and set new highs. The Dow Jones Industrial Average is composed of 30 blue-chip companies with strong balance sheets and the wherewithal to weather a storm. The health of the stock market is measured by the strength (or weakness) of big business, and this ignores a large segment of the economy.

Gold tends to respond to stock market crashes in a predictable manner. We can profit from this behavior, but in order to get the most out of our position in gold, we need to view it in terms of the greater economy. We're not just hedging against a stock market crash, but against an economic pullback. For this reason, we want to analyze gold against the GDP growth rate. Like with the stock market, the relationship tends to be inverse, yet, just as there are stages when both gold and stocks move in tandem, there are also stages when both gold and GDP move in tandem. It's the fact that gold and GDP spend more time moving in opposite directions that makes the GDP growth rate a useful economic indicator.

Gross domestic product is defined as the total monetary value of all the finished goods and services produced within a country's borders in a specific time period. Monetary value is what someone is willing to pay for the goods and services, which is different from the cost of the inputs. Nonetheless, the cost of input plays a role because goods won't be produced for long if they don't demand more than the cost of production. Gold is a commodity. In addition to serving as money and being held for investment, gold is used in the production of jewelry and certain industrial products. Gold is therefore a component of GDP, albeit an incredibly small component.

One might think that gold and GDP move hand-in-hand, not because certain uses of gold factor into GDP, but because a rise in GDP is a sign of economic prosperity. People are consuming more. There's a greater demand for jewelry and people have more money to invest. It sounds plausible, but it doesn't work that way, mainly because of the perception that gold carries. It's a defensive asset. When incomes are on the rise, people do buy more jewelry, but they also invest in equities, like stocks and real estate, rather than gold. They won't turn to gold until fear sets in. As a result, when GDP takes a hit, gold accelerates. When GDP goes up, it's gold that takes the hit.

Understanding the inverse relationship between gold and GDP is important, but simply keeping tabs on GDP isn't enough. That's because data on GDP isn't released in a timely manner, so we refer to GDP as a lagging indicator. Preliminary data comes out four weeks after the quarter ends and the final revision can take an additional two months. All the while, the price of gold can be observed in real time.

Gold is a leading indicator. At any given time, we know the price of gold. The spot price is determined by market activity that's taking place right now. When the price of gold changes, it's an immediate indication of how central banks (and to a smaller extent, individual investors) view the economic forecast. When the price of gold goes up, it's a leading indicator for economic uncertainty. When the price of gold goes down, it's a leading indicator for economic prosperity.

It's fair to conclude that the price of gold tells us more about the direction of GDP than GDP tells us about the direction of gold. But that doesn't mean a lagging indicator like GDP doesn't hold predictive value. We simply have to analyze GDP in terms of an indicator that does hold predictive value.

Instead of focusing solely on GDP, gold investors turn to the debt-to-GDP ratio. This ratio measures the total debt of a country's government against its GDP. Now, instead of looking solely at output, which is measured retroactively by GDP, we also look at the borrowing practices of the country. Debt is a current figure that is influenced by interest rates, war, recession, and a host of other factors.

A healthy debt-to-GDP ratio is less than 100%. A country whose debt is less than GDP is thought to be in a good position because it produces more than it borrows. A country with a debt-to-GDP ratio greater than 100% is also considered more likely to continue printing its fiat currency. Doing so is bearish for the currency and bullish for gold.

When GDP is viewed in terms of the nation's debt, the figure doesn't have to be timely. We're not gauging the next movement in gold based on stale GDP figures, but instead gauging a country's need for liquidity. The decision of how much money to print isn't made on a whim, and in this regard, a figure that's stale-dated by only three months should be viewed as relevant. It's not about catching gold on a dip, but instead about gauging the probability of a country printing more of their currency over the course of the next year. When the probability is high, we prepare for it by increasing our exposure to gold.

At the time of writing, the U.S. has a debt-to-GDP ratio of 108%, meaning we owe more than we produce. This isn't good, but there's worse out there. Japan has a ratio of 237%. Greece stands at 176%. Italy comes in at just under 135%. France and Spain both come in just a hair below 100%.

The U.S. debt-to-GDP ratio hasn't always been above 100%. Under favorable economic conditions, there's little reason to increase debt. Throughout the 1990s, the ratio fluctuated between 55% and 65%. The latter part of the decade saw a decrease in the debt-to-GDP ratio. This changed with the dot-com bust, the aftermath of 9/11, and the 2007-2008 financial crisis. The ratio steadily increased, reaching 83% by 2009. By 2010, it stood at 90%. From there, it continued to trend higher and now stands at 108%.

What happened to gold during this period of borrowing? Between 2006 and 2011 when the ratio increased from 62% to 95%, gold was in a ferocious bull market. Then between 2012 and 2015, the ratio stabilized at 100%—not a healthy ratio, but it persisted at this level without moving higher—and gold responded by giving back a big chunk of the gains that it earned during the bull run. Then the ratio crept higher. It hit 101%, followed by 102%, then 103%, eventually moving up to 108%. The ratio is again on the rise, this time above the 100% threshold, and gold has again entered into a bull market.

If measures are taken to get the debt-to-GDP ratio under control—that is, either decrease borrowing or increase production, or more likely a combination of the two—the price of gold should fall. If the ratio becomes even more unhealthy, the price of gold is expected to rise.

Inflation

This one's a given. We all know that gold is a hedge against inflation, so inflation is obviously an economic indicator worth watching. By monitoring changes in GDP, we essentially monitor inflation. It's not difficult, but this next statement might surprise you: inflation isn't necessarily bad. In fact, a small amount of inflation is healthy. It gives people the incentive to spend and invest their money instead of just sitting on it. In this regard, inflation keeps the economy moving in the right direction. Similarly, when a country continues to print modest amounts of their fiat currency, this is also viewed as healthy for the economy. It allows expansion to progress beyond the limitations imposed by a fixed money supply. Problems arise when too much of the fiat currency is printed, which naturally leads to an unhealthy rate of inflation. When inflation gets out of control, gold doesn't just protect our savings, but allows us to improve our financial position.

In economic terms, inflation is a quantitative measure of the increase in prices and fall in the purchasing power of a currency. The consumer used to be able to go to the grocery store and buy an eggplant for $1.00, but an eggplant of the same size now costs $1.25. That's inflation. Your money is now worth less, while the goods that you buy with your money hold the same value that they've always held. An eggplant is still an eggplant, just like coffee is still coffee. Until the eggplant's shelf life expires, it serves the same purpose that it's always served. It's still a nightshade vegetable that renews the arteries, treats dysentery, and combats varicose veins. It still gets funny looks sitting there in the produce section because most people aren't quite sure how to prepare it. The only thing that's really changed is that you now need more money to buy this strange yet amazing vegetable. The same applies to the books sitting on the shelves in your office. Their purpose doesn't change. The material in some books might become outdated, but others contain sage wisdom that never dies. The value of such books doesn't change. Instead, it's the amount of currency required to replace the books that changes.

We can dissect the effect of inflation on consumers and savers from countless perspectives. The set of glass coffee mugs you purchased right out of college has served you well. It's a good thing you haven't dropped any of them because they now cost twice as much to replace. The same can be said for your flower pots, hiking boots, bed sheets, billiard table, tea set with matching saucers, Rubik's cube, Christmas tree ornaments, those snow skis you hardly use, and the collection of junk you have stored up in the attic. It's all replaceable, but it costs more money to replace useful possessions that haven't become obsolete. The box of floppy discs sitting on your desk is now pretty much worthless, but the degree hanging on your wall would cost a lot more to earn today than it did back in . . . (*okay, we won't go there*).

So what's the solution? Should we go out and buy every product that we'll need for the rest of our lives (with the exception of electronics, produce, and other items destined to become obsolete)? Or do we invest in a suitable hedge against inflation? I vote for the hedge. It's not just because I'm a minimalist when it comes to material possessions, but because it's easier to be foresighted with investments than with goods. I have absolutely no idea how many dinner plates I'm going to break over the next ten years while entertaining friends. Should

I decide to take up juggling, the number will probably increase, so I'm not going to stock up on plates hoping to save a few bucks. Instead, I'm going to put my money into something that will maintain its value and be easy to liquidate.

Let's ignore liquidity for a minute and focus strictly on preserving value. Real estate investors know exactly what I'm talking about. Whether they realize it or not, homeowners also know what I'm talking about, but they tend to think about it in different terms. Most people buy a home not just to put a roof over their head, but because it's expected to increase in *value*. If you were to inform them that their home most likely will not increase in *value*, it might upset them. That's okay, because the fact that it won't increase in value is perfectly fine. There's something to be said for holding an asset that serves its purpose and maintains its value. At the end of the day, that's what most homes accomplish. We only think they increase in value because they increase in price.

It's going to feel good when we eventually sell our homes for more than they cost, but given that there will also be more dollars in circulation, it won't necessarily mean that the house went up in value. If there aren't any substantial improvements in the neighborhood or new companies situated nearby, or perhaps a professional sports team that popped up in our city, then the increase in the price is just that—*an increase in price*. The value hasn't changed. We still have the same home in the same neighborhood. Nothing has changed other than the fact that the dollar has declined. That's it. But the thing is, the house, which has maintained its value, isn't our only asset. We also have stocks, bonds, and savings. We have a money market account with cash set aside for a rainy day. Even as we earn interest, the purchasing power is declining. Over time, it takes more and more money to buy a second home, invest in Microsoft Corporation (MSFT), take a vacation, put children through college, and eventually retire. Our home hedges against the threat of inflation, but it's difficult to get money out of the house while we're still living in it. We need something more. We could buy a second home as a rental property. This comes with advantages and disadvantages. It's an expensive asset that requires maintenance and repairs. We'll have to take out another insurance policy and pay property taxes. But if we're able to rent the home for more than the cost of the mortgage and maintenance, then the tenants will essentially buy most of the investment for us.

The real estate market has high barriers to entry. The gold market does not. It's difficult to buy part of a house. It's even more difficult to dollar cost average into physical real estate, but it's easy to buy bullion or a gold ETF in small increments. From there, we can increase our holdings each month. The fact that gold can be purchased in small increments makes it an affordable hedge against inflation. At the time of writing, gold sells for $1,900 an ounce. A 1/10 ounce American Gold Eagle coin can be purchased in the neighborhood of $210, while a single share of the iShares Gold Trust (IAU) can be purchased at $18.11. Anyone who works for a living and strives to spend less than they make can afford to purchase gold as a hedge against inflation.

The relationship between gold and inflation is fickle. When viewed over the long-term, the relationship exhibits high positive correlation. Over the short-term, it depends on whether the rate of inflation is healthy. When the rate is somewhere in the neighborhood 3% per year, gold may or may not move in sync. It could very easily remain flat while inflation gradually moves higher. But when high inflation kicks in, gold is going to be revalued. High inflation is the impetus that forces investors to increase their exposure to gold, which in turn not only drives up the price of gold, but forces it to make up for all those years of healthy inflation when gold failed to keep pace. In essence, when inflation is high, gold not only reacts to the increase in inflation, but also makes up for lost time. This leads to a short yet fierce bull market. Those who strive to master the art of investing in gold should follow inflation closely. There are very observable indicators when inflation is on the horizon, and each should be viewed as a buy signal.

The best leading indicator we have for inflation is the commodities market. Commodities trade in a highly efficient market and their prices adjust quickly to the release of new economic data. This means the predictive value of the commodities market is stronger than that of a lagging indicator like GDP. We know what commodities and futures contracts are selling for today. It's all timely and transparent. The commodities market is also expansive and it would be next to impossible to monitor every commodity on the market. Instead, we rely on an index.

The Commodity Research Bureau (CRB) index represents the global commodities market. The index comprises a basket of 19 commodities, including energy, agriculture, industrial metals, and even precious metals. The index is updated continuously throughout the day as the price of futures contracts fluctuate.

As input prices increase, so does the price that consumers pay for most end products. An increase in the CRB index is therefore a predictor of inflation. The Consumer Price Index (CPI) can also be used to monitor changes in consumer prices, while the Producer Price Index (PPI) is used to monitor changes in input prices. In addition to commodities, the PPI also includes labor costs.

It's reassuring when multiple indexes simultaneously flash a buy signal, but investors who track multiple indicators will find that the signals rarely line up perfectly; waiting until all of your signals indicate that it's time to buy typically results in a missed buying opportunity. Increasing the information at your disposal is useful as long as it's not overwhelming.

An indication of inflation is not a guarantee of inflation. Our goal is to predict inflation before it occurs. We do so by relying on indicators, but we should also understand that no indicator is consistently accurate. The best we can do is watch, learn, and implement smart strategies. There's no right or wrong way to incorporate the movement of the CRB index into your strategy—*simply ways that make money and ways that don't.* My advice for investing based on expected inflation is to again move in shifts. When at least one of the indexes suggests a bullish position in gold, buy some gold. If the position works in your favor, buy more gold and continue to average up for however long the indicator remains bullish. Finding the proper exit point is also a matter of discretion. If you sell in shifts as gold moves higher, you can recognize gains and decrease your exposure as gold becomes riskier. If gold moves against you before you have an opportunity to liquidate your entire position, having gotten in during the early stages of the bull run increases the probability that you will only give back a portion of your gains without having to incur a loss.

The benefit of moving in shifts, as opposed to putting it all on the line as soon as you see a bullish signal and then taking it back either when you think the market can't go any higher, or worse yet, when it becomes clear that a bull run won't be materializing, applies to the use of all economic indicators. The CRB, CPI, and PPI aren't the only indexes at our disposal.

Some investors bypass the commodities indexes altogether. They instead rely on an inflation index that tracks economic variables that tend to move up or down before inflation kicks in. The Center for International Business Cycle Research (CIBCR) index consists of seven components that are believed to provide predictive value for inflation. The components include the ratio of employment to the population, the JOC industrial materials price index, the growth rate of domestic nonfinancial debt, the change in nonfuel import prices, the percent of businesses expecting higher selling prices, price diffusion experienced by manufacturers, and the rate at which suppliers fulfill orders.

Even an index geared strictly towards inflation has limitations. The goal is to maintain or even increase your exposure to gold as the index rises and then reduce or eliminate your exposure before the index retracts too heavily.

Inflation moves in stages. Paying attention to the stages will assist in finding a lucrative entry point (and also identifying when to stay away should the entry point have already passed). The first stage consists of monetary inflation. This is when the government not only continues to print its fiscal currency, but uses it to buy assets on the open market. As a result, the amount of currency in circulation inflates. Monetary inflation leads to price inflation, which in turn leads to an increase in the spot price of gold. The goal is to get in on gold before price inflation kicks in, but even if price inflation has already occurred, if gold has yet to catch up, gains can still be had.

Other leading indicators for inflation include weekly hours worked in manufacturing, orders placed for capital goods by manufacturers, and applications for unemployment insurance. Interest rates speak volumes about inflation. Interest rate cuts tend to precede periods of inflation. The deeper and more frequent the series of cuts, the stronger the indication that inflation is on the horizon.

Gold, of course, is also a leading indicator for inflation, but not a very useful one if your goal is to time your entry and exit of the gold market. Nonetheless, the expectation of inflation will send the price of gold higher. From there, the direction of gold is contingent on the relationship between expected inflation and what actually happens. This is why I recommend moving in stages. Buy in and then average up when the indicators are flashing. The goal is to recognize gains before the bull run is over. Selling in shifts is a useful approach that enables you to take gains and reduce your exposure without completely closing your position.

Keep in mind that gold trades on a global market. Global inflation, of course, will impact the price of gold. The spot price can go up as a result of inflation in other countries, which could differ from the rate of inflation in your country.

What about bonds?

In the interest of full disclosure, it's fair to admit that bonds typically serve as a better inflation hedge than gold. This is mainly due to the fact that bonds are an income generating asset. Over the past thirty years, buy-and-hold investors outperformed gold two-to-one with corporate grade bonds. The interest on bonds compounds and the impact of compounding will multiply over a long investment horizon. Stocks also tend to outperform gold over a long investment horizon, but during greater than 80% of the instances when stock returns are negative, gold returns are positive.

There's a reason that gold, when used as a hedge, should be limited to somewhere between 5% and 10% of the portfolio. While a young investor might prefer to invest strictly in equities, an aging investor should have adequate exposure to bonds and gold. The bond allocation should be significantly larger than the gold allocation. Let the compounding effect work its magic. Most of the time, you'll be happy that your gold allocation is relatively small. When your other holdings fail to do their job, you'll quickly understand the advantage of gold.

There will be intervals when gold outperforms bonds. Typically, the bond interest paid during these isolated periods is negligible, like it is at the time of writing. The asset allocator is guaranteed the best of both worlds, albeit in modest proportions.

What about deflation?

Okay. So we know that the spot price of gold is strongly correlated with periods of high inflation. The greater the inflation, the stronger the bull market for gold. But what about deflation? It seems logical that in a deflationary environment, gold would do just the opposite, but it doesn't. Gold reacts to extremes. If there's high inflation or high deflation, gold goes up. Gold soared during the Great Depression. The stock market may have crashed, but gold mining stocks provided strong returns. Remember, gold isn't just a hedge against inflation, it's a hcdgc against fear.

Quantitative easing

Quantitative easing is a form of monetary policy in which a central bank prints currency and then uses it to purchase long-term securities on the open market in order to increase the money supply. The impact on gold is predictable: the amount of money in circulation increases, which sends the price of gold higher.

Not surprising, quantitative easing is a precursor for inflation. When the money supply increases, the cost of goods and services inevitably goes up. There's a two-pronged effect on gold: (1) when the Fed Chair simply utters the words quantitative easing, there's a dramatic increase in the price of gold, and (2) the inflation that follows will lead to further increases.

It's difficult to time an announcement. When quantitative easing is announced, you're either invested in gold or you're not. The asset allocator is in a good position to reap this reward. The market timer might also be invested in gold. If you're not invested in gold prior to the announcement, don't let the sudden jump in price lead you to believe that it's too late to get in on gold. There's a strong probability that inflation will follow and gold will continue to rise.

Interest rates

There's an inverse relationship between interest rates and gold. Gold tends to outperform when interest rates are low and underperform when interest rates are high. It makes sense because gold competes with bonds for space in the portfolio. When most investors assess their tolerance for risk, the question they're asking themselves is, how much of the portfolio should I allocate to equities? The remainder of the portfolio gets split between safe haven assets like bonds and gold. The larger the yield on bonds, the more attractive they are. When rates are so low that yields are negligible, bonds lose their appeal. In a low interest rate environment, investors aren't sacrificing a stream of income when they make room for gold. As a result, gold tends to increase in price as interest rates are lowered. On top of that, a low interest rate is a precursor for high inflation; *all the more reason to make a side bet on gold!*

It's tempting to take a contrarian approach and invest in gold when interest rates are high. We anticipate that rates will eventually get cut and this will cause the spot price of gold to go up. So if we get in while interest rates are still high, we catch the entire gold bull as cuts are implemented. This might seem logical, but it's a bad idea. There's no ceiling on how high interest rates can go. Just because rates are high doesn't mean they'll be cut anytime in the foreseeable future. In the 1980s interest rates were outrageous. The average mortgage rate in 1981 was 17%. Can you imagine? At the time I was still learning to say the word "mortgage" and it would be another twenty years before I even considered buying a house. I'm ecstatic that rates have returned to reasonable levels. But it's different when you're on the receiving end of an interest payment. Rates progressively fell throughout the 1980s, but were still high enough to provide a sizable stream of income. Naturally, bonds were more attractive than gold, which can be seen in the spot price of gold. It's one of the factors that played into the 26-year dry spell. Throughout the 1980s, investors had to choose between earning double-digit interest income on their bonds or watching their investment in gold move sideways.

Interest rates might not have a ceiling, but they do have a floor. Governments will lower rates in an effort to stimulate economic activity, but there's only so much economic activity that can be stimulated by keeping rates low. Eventually, a low rate does nothing more than punish savers and retirees. We can argue that when rates have been cut to near-zero, they have no place to go but up. And most of the time that's what happens. A negative interest rate is possible, but undesirable. It gives banks added incentive to issue loans because it costs them money to sit on cash. If you think the subprime mortgage crisis of 2007-2008 was bad, imagine what could happen when banks are required to pay interest on the money they aren't lending out. This type of situation will send the price of gold higher. The U.S. has never implemented negative interest rates, but they have been used elsewhere in the world, including Denmark, Japan, Hungry, Sweden, Switzerland, and the European Union. At the timing of writing, we're in the midst of the coronavirus pandemic, and the need for negative interest rates in the U.S. is being discussed. If enacted, the bull run in gold is likely to become even more bullish.

It's advantageous to invest in gold while rates are low, even if there's no reason to believe that they will keep going lower (or even turn negative). That's because the rate does not have to keep trending lower in order to send gold higher. Once rates are low enough, gold will keep going higher even as rates begin to rise. When interest rates move from 0.25% to 0.5% and then to 0.75%, the trend is upward, but the rate still isn't high enough to attract bond investors. At this level, gold can keep going higher. It's not until bonds pay enough interest to catch everyone's attention that we really need to worry about gold.

When specifically to get out of gold is a factor of both the level that rates have risen to and the projected outlook for additional hikes.

The role of hyperinflation

If you were to wake up tomorrow morning and see that the price of gold had risen by 5.62% and had no additional information, you might think there's a problem in the financial community, like a war has started or we're entering a period of hyperinflation. While these types of events are disconcerting, you might also pat yourself on the back for having sought the protection of gold. That's the stigma of a safe haven.

Now, what if gold goes up much faster than that? What if it doubles in price over just a few months? It's happened before and it could conceivably happen again. While this is good for the gold investor, it's also a sign that something is fundamentally wrong with the global economy. Gold is a hedge against high inflation, which means it's also a hedge against hyperinflation.

I'm going to use the term hyperinflation loosely. It's defined as a 50% increase in prices that occurs over the course of a month. The U.S. has never actually experienced hyperinflation. The closest we've come was during the Civil War when the price of goods increased by 117% between 1861 and 1865. A loose definition of hyperinflation—which many investors use—is inflation that exceeds what is typical for a given economy during inflationary periods. That's how we'll be using the term in this section. It simply refers to inflation that is unprecedentedly high for the U.S. economy.

Is hyperinflation bad? It is for the economy. If you're an investor, then the answer depends on how much gold you're exposed to. Hyperinflation is what ultimately sends gold through the roof. While gold is a store of value during an economic downturn, it serves as a receiver of wealth when the downturn gives way to hyperinflation.

People get scared during a recession. They stop spending and start saving. Even those who lack basic money management skills will start to save—*that's the power of fear*—and this change in consumer habits will lead to a period of deflation. The impact of a large portion of the population cutting back on their spending as they ramp up their savings exacerbates the recession. Equities are likely to take a hit, but the spot price of gold is going to go up. A period of stabilization will follow as we work our way out of the recession. Fear begins to subside as the unemployment rate declines. People are no longer clinging to every penny they can find, but they're still not spending like they used to. That will change when the fear completely subsides. When people do start spending again, it will exceed normal consumption. Imagine if you've gone two full days without water (I'm not recommending you try this, but just imagine). When you're finally able to drink again, are you going to have a little or a lot? Water is a basic need, but the same concept applies when people are denied luxuries for long periods. Once the fear completely subsides, they don't go out and spend a little, *they go out and spend a lot!* How much they spend depends on how hard the recession impacted them. Those who got scared and saved without actually losing their job or experiencing a decrease in their income have a lot of savings stacked up. They're in a position to really spend. Those who suffered a job loss but have since found new employment might feel entitled to reward themselves with some discretionary spending. It's different for everyone. The common factor is that we're all suddenly in a position to spend more than we did before. The money has to go somewhere. Some people are going to buy stocks while others buy goods. Both of these actions have a positive effect on the economy, which further alleviates the residue of lingering fear and leads to even more spending. This rapid increase in spending after a prolonged period of stagnation leads to hyperinflation. Stocks are again going up. The recovery has started. But gold is now doing more than just storing value in the face of opposition—*it's shooting for the sky!* Our dollars are now worth a lot less, which means it's going to take a lot more of them to buy gold. The funny thing is, a lot of people aren't even paying attention to gold. The stock market is finally back on track, and that's where everyone turns their attention. The fact that gold is outpacing equities by leaps and bounds seldom receives the media attention it deserves.

Gold is going to be embraced by those who understand the economic events that create demand, but it's going to be forgotten as soon as those economic events subside. When the bull run is over and gold falls into bear territory, there's no telling how long it will be until gold comes back—*who knows, 26 years?* It's not a bad thing, unless you're adamant on holding gold for the long haul. If you are, it means you're going to miss out on what everyone else considers the good times. There's nothing worse than suffering through a bear market in gold while the neighbors are seeing huge gains on their income-producing investments. It's just a horrible place to be. That's why you want to sell in shifts as gold advances, rather than trying to call the top. When hyperinflation sets in, gold has the potential to rally hard, but bull markets in gold never end well. When you ride one, you're playing hot potato. The economy doesn't have to enter a state of hyperinflation in order for gold to work its magic, but when it does, the magic is all the more powerful. If you're still holding on after inflation stabilizes, your investment is going to take a hit.

Chapter 8: When Art Meets Science

I'm a firm believer that everyone should subscribe to the science of investing in gold. The art, on the other hand, is for those who want to do more. The artist should still contribute to their 401(k), they should follow the basic principles of modern portfolio theory, but still, *they want more*. Investing becomes their hobby. It's an endeavor that they allocate a sizable portion of their discretionary income towards, and they . . .

. . . *they place side bets*. That's what the artist should be doing. Don't put 40% of your net worth into gold because you're confident in your ability to time the market. If you're wrong, it's going to hurt. Instead, allocate maybe 70% of your discretionary income to an investment that you have confidence in. Or 50%. Or maybe 85%. It's up to you. The point that I'm trying to make is that the art of investing in gold is about more than just timing entry and exit points. Just like with the science, it's also about controlling for risk. We do this first by keeping our hands away from our retirement savings, and second, by determining how much of our discretionary income we're willing to risk on a specific investment.

If we want, we can do even more. All we have to do is implement aspects of the science into our side bets. With modern portfolio theory, we strive to earn the highest return possible for a given level of risk. When making a side bet, as opposed to investing our retirement savings, we rightfully have a higher tolerance for risk. If we're bullish on gold, we might decide to invest some of our discretionary income in a gold ETF, but we also might decide to hedge this position with a 10% stock allocation. You read that right, we're now using stocks as a modest hedge against our bullish position in gold, and we're going to rebalance between the two for however long we remain bullish. Essentially, we've now combined the art and science of investing in gold. Once we've had our fill and are ready to stop riding the bull, we'll do something else.

This isn't the only way to combine art with science. In fact, the science gets a lot more interesting as we explore different ways to rebalance between gold and other asset classes. Let's have a look.

Dow/Gold Ratio

It's intuitive to measure gold in dollars. That's how we measure just about everything. When we buy jeans, we want to know how many dollars they cost. When we go to college, tuition is expressed in terms of dollars. When we buy an investment, it costs dollars. When we sell an investment, we receive dollars. It's natural to think this way, but we're going to change our way of thinking in an effort to determine if gold is priced at a discount.

Gold is a tricky investment because it's difficult to measure its intrinsic value. We can't make predictions about future earnings and then discount them back to present value because there aren't any earnings. The spot price of gold is a product of demand. When buyers exceed sellers, the price goes up. When sellers exceed buyers, the price goes down. We know how the market prices gold at any given point in time, but what we really want is a method for determining whether or not the market is right. Put differently, we want to know if gold is over- or underpriced relative to other assets. If it's underpriced, we buy. If it's overpriced, we sell. It sounds simple because it is simple. All we need is a metric that tells us whether or not gold is currently cheap or expensive.

The Dow/gold ratio measures the price of gold in terms of large cap stocks. At the time of writing, the Dow Jones Industrial Average is at 28,000 and gold is selling for $1,900 per ounce.

The Dow/gold ratio is calculated as follows:

28,000 / 1,900 = 14.74

We should stop trying to determine if gold is fairly priced in terms of dollars because dollars are a meaningless metric for evaluating the value of anything. The number of dollars in circulation keeps increasing. It's more efficient to measure gold against an asset that we could have purchased in place of gold. If we're holding gold and decide that we'd rather invest in the Dow Jones Industrial Average, we have to sell gold for dollars and then use those dollars to buy an ETF that tracks the Dow Jones Industrial Average. If we execute the transactions before the dollar loses value—that is, if we leisurely execute one transaction and then the next, all before the dollars currently being printed cause inflation—then it doesn't really matter what the dollar is worth. We've swapped gold for stocks. That's it.

When we stop thinking in terms of dollars and measure the price of gold in terms of the Dow/gold ratio, what we're really measuring is the purchasing power of gold. When the price of gold goes up as the stock market goes down, our ability to invest in the stock market increases. We can now buy a greater number of shares in the Dow for however much gold we're holding. When stocks go up as the price of gold declines, the result is just the opposite. Our stake in gold is now going to buy fewer shares of the Dow. That is, of course, assuming we're invested in gold as this happens. If we're invested in stocks instead, the act of stocks rising as gold declines enables us to buy a lot more gold.

We've already established that gold is not a buy-and-hold asset (unless it's held as a modest hedge in a fully-diversified portfolio). When buying gold for protection (and profit) during an economic downturn, the big question is, when do I hold gold and when do I hold cash? That's how most investors think. An even better question is, when do I hold gold and when do I hold the Dow? If we get this question right, our propensity to build wealth increases. If we get it wrong, then we'd have been better off holding cash.

A smart investor knows how to use probability to her advantage. If we're going to trade back and forth between gold and the Dow, then we need a way to measure probability. That's exactly what the Dow/gold ratio does. When the ratio is at 5 or lower, the Dow is considered cheap and gold is considered expensive. When the ratio is at 15 or higher, the Dow is considered expensive and gold is considered cheap. At the time of writing, the ratio is at 14.74. Gold is already two years into a bull run and the stock market is considered expensive in terms of P/E ratio.

Conventional wisdom dictates that when the ratio falls below 5, it's time to sell gold and buy stocks. When the ratio gets up above 15, it's time to sell stocks and buy gold. Historically, that's how the ratio has been used. If we go back 100 years, we see that this approach provides three opportunities to swap gold for stocks and three opportunities to swap stocks for gold. Had we been alive and invested for the entirety of this period, we'd all be very rich. If we had waited until 1996 to buy in, we'd all be sitting on a pile of gold that's tripled in value, but still, we could have done better. The ratio proceeds to fall to 7 without actually reaching 5. Had we sold gold for the Dow at this point, we'd have been in a better position as stocks recovered. It's difficult to time a market that comes close to hitting a buy signal without actually hitting the signal. That's what makes investing in gold an art.

Dow/Gold Ratio

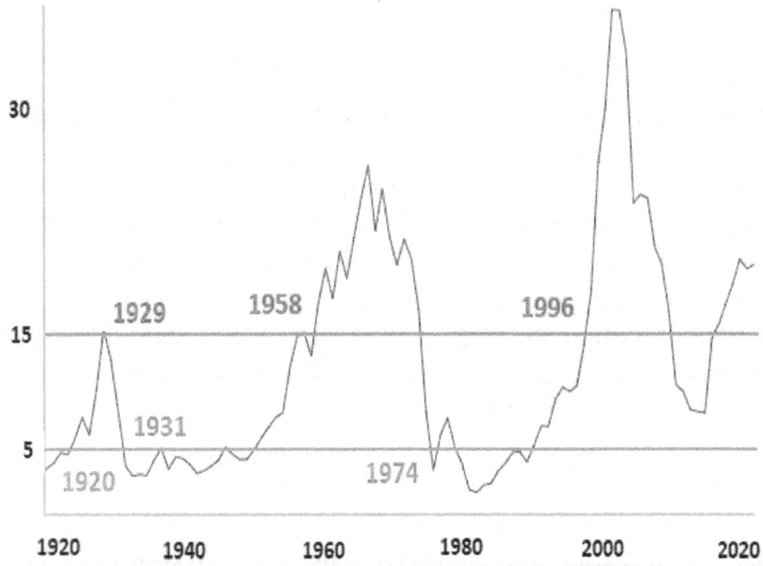

You don't have to be a professional analyst to see that stocks, when measured in gold, progressively become more expensive. Each time the ratio peaks, it's significantly higher than before. When measured in gold, investors are paying more for stocks today than they have in the past. The last time the ratio fell below 5 was in 1987. During the dot-com bust, the 2007-2008 financial crisis, and the coronavirus crash, stocks declined in value, but when measured in gold, they remained more expensive than they were in the 1980s.

This might sound familiar. We discussed a similar phenomenon in *Beating The Market*. We used the CAPE ratio to determine if stocks were cheap or expensive when measured as a ratio of earnings. The historic average PE ratio for the S&P 500 is 16, and the stock market is considered more or less efficient when the ratio fluctuates between 12 and 20. Stocks are considered cheap when the ratio falls below 12 (or so) and they're considered expensive when the ratio rises above 20.

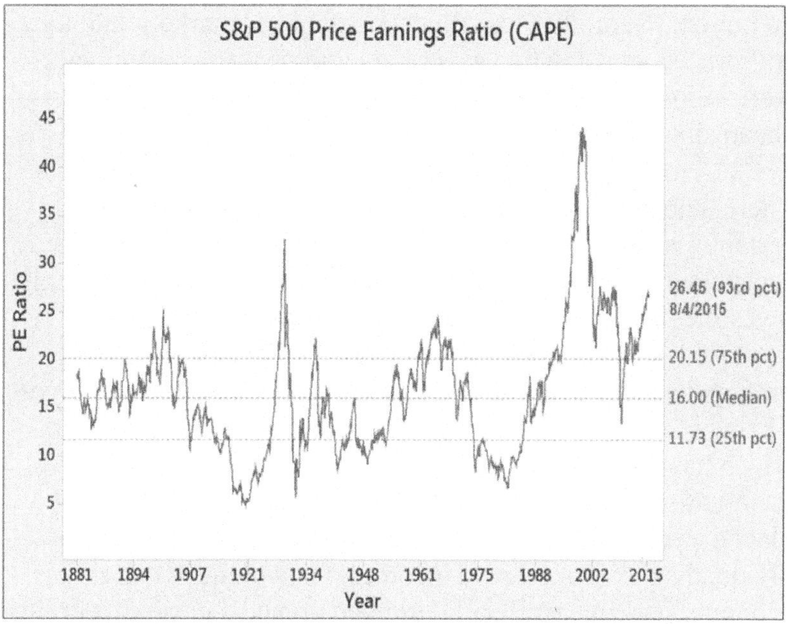

The ratio has been above 20 for a long time, ever since the 2007-2008 financial crisis. Before that, when the dot-com bubble burst, the ratio didn't even fall below 20. Even though the stock market crashed, stocks were so expensive before the crash that they didn't look like much of a bargain after the crash. It took the global financial crisis of 2007-2008 to pull stocks down to a level that's considered cheap by historic standards. The coronavirus crash mimicked the bursting of the dot-com bubble. Stocks were so expensive before the crash that they still didn't look like much of a bargain when the market bottomed in March of 2020. The recovery was fierce and investors who bought at the bottom recognized large returns in a short amount of time. We're not out of the woods yet. It will be interesting to see if the V-shaped recovery continues or if the stock market takes a second dip.

Regardless of how you measure the price of stocks, either in terms of dollars or gold, investors have started paying more for stocks at all stages of the economic cycle. It's been decades since stocks were truly so cheap that they really had no place to go but up. Naturally, we still encounter bear markets, and they still drag stocks down to a price level that's lower than they were before the bear market, but stocks haven't been truly cheap since the early 1980s.

There's no single explanation. The advent of the 401(k) certainly had an impact. As defined contribution plans gained acceptance, more and more Americans started making monthly investments in the stock market. As the number of buyers increased, so did the prices. The advent of online discount brokers has had a similar effect. It's never been easier to invest. The newfound convenience has led to an increase in demand, which has had an obvious impact on price. Overreliance on quantitative easing and maintaining low interest rates has also played a role. When interest rates are low, investors turn to dividend stocks for passive income. Many believe that the economy is being artificially propped up and a crash that brings stock valuations down to early 1980s levels is long overdue. Should that happen, gold is likely to outperform. The savvy investor will sell gold to buy stocks after the asset classes have moved in opposite directions. Those who use gold as a portfolio hedge will do so systematically through the process of rebalancing.

With the Dow/gold ratio at 14.74 and the CAPE ratio at 31.34, conventional wisdom suggests that we're better off making a side bet in gold and that we shouldn't switch to stocks until the Dow/gold ratio falls back to 5. This might be the way to go, but we have to remember that the environment keeps changing. Every time the Dow/gold ratio peaks, it does so at a much higher level. Last time it fell, it only went to 7 instead of 5. This begs the question, how do we invest *today* based on the Dow/gold ratio? I have two answers. The first is a quasi-conservative approach that offers attractive results. The second is a more aggressive approach that offers even better results (unless your timing is off, in which case the results could be detrimental).

Quasi-conservative approach

A strategy that works consistently will never require you to call the turning points of a market. It's just too hard. Sure, the Dow/gold ratio has formed a pattern of setting new highs, but we're not going to try to predict the next turning point. Instead, we're going to pair our bets by implementing a strategy based on modern portfolio theory. We're going to make our investments, allow the markets to move through their cycles, and take gains systematically through rebalancing. It's the same concept that we apply to our retirement savings. The overarching difference is that we're going to increase our exposure to gold. This essentially combines the art and science of investing in gold.

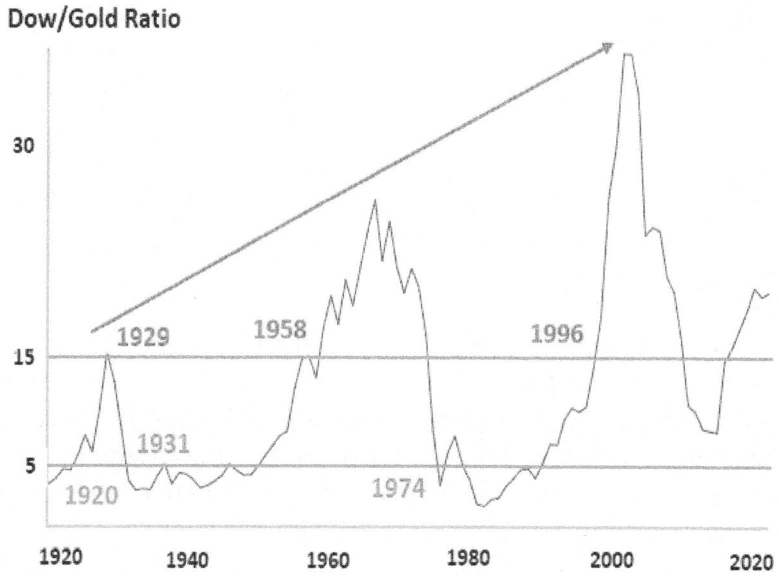

As a side bet, we're going to buy just two assets: (1) an ETF that tracks the Dow Jones Industrial Average, and (2) an ETF that holds gold. We'll put 50% of our capital in stocks and 50% in gold. Then we wait. We give our holdings an opportunity to move. If gold goes up and stocks go down, we'll sell some of our gold allocation (at a gain) and buy more of the Dow (at a discount). Now we're back to a 50/50 allocation. Then we wait some more. If stocks go up and gold goes down, then we do just the opposite: we sell stocks and buy gold. We're again back to a 50/50 allocation. As we repeat the process, we systematically trade back and forth between the two funds based on which asset class is selling at a premium and which can be picked up at a discount. Not only that, but the constituents of the Dow all pay dividends, so we'll reinvest our dividend income along the way. This creates a compounding effect that we can't get from gold alone.

Over extended periods of time, we expect to see large gains, especially when both asset classes trend upwards in alternating intervals. When that doesn't happen and one of the asset classes takes a damaging hit, the other asset class serves as a hedge. In the long-run, this is actually good. Whichever fund takes the hit will be selling at a deep discount. We'll sell into the strength of the advancing asset class and buy into the weakness of the opposing asset class. We're again back to a 50/50 allocation. After more time passes, we do it again. The benefit of both rebalancing and reinvesting the dividend income will continue to compound for however long we practice the strategy.

A 50/50 split is quasi-conservative. When stocks are on the rise, it might feel like the gold allocation is holding us back, but the true benefit emerges as we allow each of our holdings to work through their prolonged secular cycles. Short-term volatility will enable us to sell the peaks and buy the valleys, but the long-term movements are even more profound.

When it comes to a rebalancing strategy, the behavior of gold in relation to the Dow Jones Industrial average over the past five years is exactly what we want. Both asset classes trend upwards, but they do so with alternating advances. Over the first couple years, we see gold and the Dow cross paths several times as they fight for the lead.

We don't have to catch the tops and bottoms of each gyration in order for the strategy to work. We just need to be in the ballpark. I recommend rebalancing every three to four months.

I'm tempted to say that you can't go wrong with this approach, but that's not entirely true. If you see things through, even when one of the assets classes enters a painfully long bear market, you'll be fine. The U.S. stock market has always recovered and then gone on to set new highs. Gold will likely do the same, but we can't ignore the fact that gold once spent 26 years in bear territory. That's why the science of investing in gold indicates that no more than 10% of the portfolio should be allocated to gold. What we're doing here is blending art and science. We preserve some of the science by maintaining a balanced portfolio. While there's still a degree of inherent safety to this approach, we make it an art by upping the gold allocation to an amount that really pays off when gold advances, even though the downside can be ugly. With the quasi-conservative approach, we simply maintain our allocation and see things through. If we want to avoid the lengthy periods of time when gold wallows in bear territory, we need to rely more heavily on the art. To do so, we turn to the aggressive approach.

Aggressive approach

When held for extended periods of time, both gold and the stock market are expected to beat inflation, yet they both exhibit vastly different behavior. On days when the stock market is down, gold tends to be up. On days when gold is down, the stock market tends to be up. It's not uncommon for both asset classes to follow the same long-term trend while exhibiting short-term movements in opposing directions. At other times, it's the long-term trend that moves in opposing directions.

When both asset classes are accelerating, the act of rebalancing leads to larger gains. When the long-term trend for both asset classes is down, the act of rebalancing helps contain the losses. It forces the investor to sell the asset that put up a better fight in order to invest in the asset that just took the harder beating.

On average, the Dow Jones Industrial Average experiences shorter bear markets than gold. This begs the question, is a 50/50 split the best way to trade the Dow/gold ratio?

The benefit to maintaining at least some exposure to each asset class at all times is that it mitigates losses when markets don't behave as expected. No matter how confident you are with your economic analysis, there will be times when the markets surprise you. It goes with the territory of being an investor. We don't have to stick with a 50/50 split, but it would be foolish to go all-in on gold just because we see inflation coming. If we're confident that gold is going to take off and leave stocks in the dust, we can overweight in favor of gold. If we're bullish on the stock market and bonds are paying high enough interest that no one really cares about gold, we can overweight in favor of stocks. We're now relying more heavily on our ability to time the market, but we maintain a hedge while doing so.

Historically, when the Dow/gold ratio fell below 5, it was viewed as a signal to sell gold and buy stocks. When the ratio rose above 15, it was viewed as a signal to sell stocks and buy gold. In recent decades, we see that the movements don't conform to this range as neatly as we'd like. The ratio might fall to 7 without going as low as 5, and it can easily pass 15 and keep going, even passing 30. It seems foolish to implement a strategy that requires us to stop on a dime and completely switch from one asset class to another. Instead, as the ratio moves lower, perhaps around 8, we increase our stock allocation as we decrease our gold allocation. Maybe we'll go with a 60/40 split. If the ratio changes directions and reverts higher, we're now in a better position for the ride. But if it goes lower first, say around 6, we can widen the split to 70/30. By doing so, we still sell gold to buy stocks, but we don't completely eliminate our exposure to gold. The trend isn't going to change directions just because we changed our position, but the ratio is in the neighborhood where the direction is likely to change nonetheless. Whenever the change comes, we'll be in prime position to let stocks work their magic.

The ratio will eventually rise and we can expect the pattern to persist. As the ratio rises to 10, 11, 12, and even 13, we're more heavily weighted in favor of stocks and it works to our advantage. Once the ratio passes 15, we might decide to adjust our holdings. It's time to sell some stocks to buy more gold. We might move from a 60/40 split to a 40/60 split. This preemptively puts us in a good possession for when the trend reverses and the ratio decreases. We're not going to get upset if the ratio goes higher first. We still have plenty of exposure to stocks. Once the ratio crosses 20, we might decide to widen our split to 30/70, putting us in an even better position for the eventual reversal. Then we wait.

By adjusting our allocation based on where the ratio has moved, we essentially buy and sell in shifts. As the ratio increases, we sell more and more stocks in favor of gold. As the ratio decreases, we sell more and more gold in favor of stocks. At no point do we tell ourselves that stocks have gone as high as they're going to go and then switch entirely to gold. We also never tell ourselves that gold has gone as high as it's going to go and then switch entirely to stocks. We maintain at least a modest hedge at all times, but we systematically swap the asset classes that we're betting on, rather than hedging with, as the ratio moves from one end of the spectrum to the other.

How you adjust your holdings as the ratio oscillates is entirely at your discretion. The allocations presented above are purely for the sake of illustration. In practice, you'll be the one reading the economic indicators and observing the Dow/gold ratio. Every investor has a different style. On top of that, the economic environment is in a constant state of evolution. With time, the range that the Dow/gold ratio fluctuates within can progressively trend higher. Or the ratio might fall back below 5 and take a really long time to revert. Your guess is as good as mine. You'll want to take other factors into consideration so that your guess is an educated guess. Where does the debt-to-GDP ratio stand and in what direction is it trending? How long ago was the last bear market in stocks? Do stocks look expensive? What's the volatility index doing? Is fear starting to get to people? Are they talking about it at the water cooler? How much gold are central banks buying? Are interest rates high or low? What about cryptocurrencies? Are investors starting to take them more seriously? Are cryptocurrencies starting to compete with bonds and gold for the portion of the portfolio that isn't allocated to equities? This is just a sample of the questions you should be asking as you trade the Dow/gold ratio. It's what makes investing in gold an art.

Gold/Silver Ratio

The Dow Jones Industrial Average isn't the only investment that can be rebalanced against gold. Some investors pay more attention to the gold/silver ratio than they do to the Dow/gold ratio. When rebalancing between gold and silver, the objective is more about increasing your exposure to gold than it is about large gains. Once the exposure has been increased, the gains follow naturally when the fear of inflation sets in.

A lot of investors assume that gold and silver exhibit strong positive correlation because they're both precious metals. It's a reasonable assumption, but if we look closer at how each is used, we see that the forces of supply and demand affect them differently. In other words, gold and silver serve two distinctly different purposes. Gold is money. It has other applications, such as jewelry and dental fillings, but these applications are a small part of the demand for gold. Silver, on the other hand, has many applications. It's one of the best-known electrical conductors. Demand for this use is expected to remain strong. Silver is also used in photography, silverware, jewelry, and a variety of industrial applications. Like gold, it's used to make coins, so it does serve as money, but less than 25% of the demand for silver is for coins and investments. Silver tends to function as a commodity while gold functions as money. They don't rise and fall in price at the same time. The investor who takes a sum of money, places 50% in gold and 50% in silver, and then rebalances several times a year will find himself trading back and forth between the two.

By now the concept of rebalancing should be second nature and you're probably sick of reading about it. Nonetheless, when gold goes up by more than silver (or declines by less than silver), the act of rebalancing forces the investor to sell gold to buy silver. And vice-versa. Then we repeat, repeat, and repeat. The long-term effect is that we increase our holdings of both gold and silver. This time around, we're not rebalancing against the Dow, which means we're not rebalancing against an asset class that we expect to always recover from a crash and then go on to set a new high. It's possible for precious metals to experience bull runs that don't even come close to setting a new high. Or they could just as easily move sideways for years. We can make our predictions and time our entry points, but we can't just buy and hold either metal with the expectation that large gains will follow.

When we rebalance between gold and silver, we mitigate the opportunity cost that precious metals might move sideways for extended periods of time. We don't just buy gold and sit on it. We don't just buy silver and sit on it. Instead, we allocate a sum of money to each asset, say 50/50, or maybe 70/30, or whatever we want it to be. Then, while other precious metals investors twiddle their thumbs, we increase the size of our holdings by rebalancing the portfolio. The pie gets bigger as we trade back and forth. When a bull market comes along and pushes one (or both) of these precious metals higher, we reap the rewards.

I stated before that gold is rarely the asset of choice amongst value investors. If you buy gold just because it appears cheap, you might end up waiting a really long time before it moves higher, and the stock market could advance by leaps and bounds, or at least pay dividends, while you wait. If you're trading the gold/silver ratio, it's okay to break this rule. When gold (or better yet, gold and silver) looks cheap, that's the time to start. It may or may not move higher in the near future, but it will exhibit some volatility, and rebalancing with silver as it exhibits this volatility enables you to increase the size of your holdings. That's all you have to do. Trade back and forth as you rebalance. Let a year pass. Then two. Three. Five. Eight. You've significantly increased the size of your holdings, even if the change in spot price isn't spectacular. And that's okay, because when precious metals rally, they rally hard. All those years of increasing your stake is going to pay off. This is a game you want to start playing when precious metals look cheap. Wait for the next bull run, and then make a point of getting out before the bull calls it quits. If gold and silver don't rally at the same time, even better. You'll sell the metal that rallies first and buy more of the metal that rallies second. Then, make sure you get out of the second metal before it's too late. When gold and silver crash, they crash hard.

If you've realized strong gains and are starting to question how much steam is left in the precious metals, it's okay to dump silver and switch to the Dow/gold ratio. This is a safer game to play through all stages of the economic cycle. It also enables you to start earning some dividend income. When precious metals look cheap, there's an advantage to playing the gold/silver ratio. After it pays off and the playing field becomes less predictable, the Dow/gold ratio enables you to then hedge your bets between stocks and gold.

Chapter 9: Gold Mining Stocks

I keep alluding to this chapter because gold mining stocks aren't just interesting investments, they're also a unique tool that can be used to build wealth quickly. Just like gold, it's a matter of timing, and discretion is a must. There are times when gold mining stocks provide better returns than gold, but what outperforms on the upside often proves disastrous on the downside. If your timing isn't right, a lot of money can be lost by investing in gold mining stocks. It all comes down to the fact that gold mining stocks function as a leveraged investment.

Naturally, the stock price of a company that mines a commodity is going to be highly correlated with the spot price of the commodity. When it comes to the art of investing in gold, gold mining stocks can be used to earn huge returns during specific intervals of the economic cycle. Outside of those specific intervals, gold mining stocks make for lousy investments. There isn't a nicer way to say it.

The art of investing in gold mining stocks is challenging. We essentially take everything we know about investing in gold and combine it with stock evaluation. Now we're looking at companies that have the potential to be mismanaged and file for bankruptcy. We're also looking at companies that have the potential to outperform the competition. When proper market timing and stock selection are combined, huge rewards can be had. When the elements aren't combined appropriately, the damage can be devastating. This is the nature of a leveraged investment.

Gold mining stocks are more volatile than gold. That's okay, as long as we understand how these stocks function. I've cautioned before that gold, when used to hedge a properly diversified portfolio, should comprise no more than 10% of the holdings. When we substitute gold mining stocks for gold, the proportions change. With greater volatility comes greater responsibility. It sounds like something you might read in a

Spiderman comic, but it's true. The scientist might decide to limit her exposure to gold mining stocks to just 5% of the portfolio. The artist might allocate no more than 35% of his capital to gold mining stocks when trading the Dow/gold [miners] ratio. Should an investor decide to hold both gold and gold mining companies, which in my opinion isn't a bad idea, particularly when fear is strong and inflation is on the horizon, she should adjust her allocation accordingly. You'll understand why as we discuss gold mining stocks as a leveraged investment. There's also a chart to illustrate the type of fire that we're playing with.

Gold Miners as a Leveraged Investment

The traditional method of investing with leverage is to secure a loan from your broker, which enables you to control more shares of stock than the amount of money that you've invested can actually buy. As a result, the gains and losses are both amplified. A requirement of the loan will be that you maintain a specified margin requirement. If the stock declines in price and forces you below the margin requirement, you'll be required to contribute more capital to the account. If you fail to do so, the broker is then at liberty to close your position. When we say that gold mining stocks function as a leveraged investment, we aren't actually buying on margin. There's no loan involved. Instead, we simply mean that investing in gold miners is akin to investing in gold, except that the gains and losses are amplified.

Unlike gold bullion, gold mining stocks are not a safe haven. If you're looking for a store of value, look elsewhere. As mentioned above, these are volatile investments. The upside will make you salivate, but the downside is going to make your stomach churn. These companies mine a commodity that doesn't function like a normal commodity. It functions first as money and second as an investment. It's use as a commodity is accounted for further down the line. When there's a bull run on gold, these companies really make out. When gold is in a bear market, the cost of mining gold doesn't go down, but stays relatively constant. The only thing that goes down is the price the commodity sells for. During a lengthy bear market, the damage can be severe.

If you're already a savvy gold investor, this following statement might make you cringe. That's okay. I'm going to make it purely for the sake of illustration and then revise it to something that better fits your understanding of input costs. Here goes:

Gold mining stocks function as a leveraged investment because the cost of mining gold is static, while the selling price of gold is volatile.

Gold mining companies incur a variety of costs. Before they even start drilling, there's the excavation cost of finding gold. Then there's labor, machinery, and energy costs. There's also the standard overhead cost that just about every company incurs. All of these costs are incurred before they even have an opportunity to sell their first ounce of gold. If the spot price of gold goes up, these costs are still incurred. Worse yet, if the spot price of gold goes down, the gold miner still has to pay the piper. The current trend in the spot price is decoupled from the input costs. The cost of mining gold is what it is. Sometimes this is good. When fear sets in and the spot price of gold rises, the input costs remain relatively idle. When the bull run ends and a ferocious bear comes out of the woods, the spot price drops, but the input costs again remain idle. Thus, an investor can assume a leveraged position in gold simply by investing in gold miners; they don't have to take out a loan, pay interest, maintain their margin requirement, or worry about losing more than the amount they invested. The extraneous hazards of trading on margin are mostly avoided.

If you're already entrenched in this facet of investing, or perhaps own or work for a mining company, you're probably rolling your eyes and telling yourself that the input costs of mining gold are anything but static. Miners don't work for free and many of them unionize. They want to see their income increase with inflation, if not more. The cost of machinery is fixed at the time of purchase, but what about the cost of maintenance or buying new machinery? These costs aren't completely fixed. And let's not forget the cost of energy. This is one of the largest input costs that gold miners incur. The amount of oil used is directly proportional to the amount of time spent drilling. The deeper they have to drill to find gold, the more expensive the extraction. On top of that, the cost of oil fluctuates. Anyone who's ever maintained a long-term position in Exxon Mobil Corporation (XOM) can confirm that the price of oil is anything but stable. In many ways, owning shares in an energy company serves as a leveraged investment in crude oil, just as owning shares in a gold mining company serves as a leveraged investment in gold. When the cost of oil goes up, it eats directly into the gold miners' bottom line.

Gold mining companies can take measures to protect themselves. They can use futures contracts to lock in the price that they pay for oil. They can also lock in the price at which they sell gold. This is an example of futures contracts being used for their intended purpose, rather than for speculation. But during a prolonged bear market, even this approach won't protect them indefinitely. When the bull is fierce, these companies want the highest dollar they can earn, not the safety of a futures contract. When the bull ends, some companies are better prepared than others. With time, the movement of gold is real and the impact is felt by all.

So if the input costs are anything but fixed, why am I making this inherently flawed analogy? It's because when the movements are extreme, this analogy isn't flawed. When gold enters bull territory, it moves quickly and will outpace any increases to the cost of mining. When you flip the coin over, just the opposite happens. During a vicious bear market, the spot price of gold is going to fall. The input prices probably won't, but if they do, they're not going to fall nearly as fast. Leverage is thus achieved, even as the cost of mining fluctuates.

It's during prolonged bear markets that the analogy of gold miners as a leveraged investment falls apart. When gold has fallen but then moves sideways for extended durations, the cost of mining can fluctuate more than the spot price of gold. It's during the extremes, when gold is on a fierce bull run or has succumbed to a ferocious bear, that an investment in gold miners tends to function as a leveraged investment. For this reason, the art of investing in gold mining stocks is riskier than the art of investing in gold. It should be pursued with caution.

The Science of Investing in Gold Mining Stocks

Let's ignore stock selection for a minute and focus on the science of investing in gold mining stocks. The process is exactly the same as using gold to hedge the portfolio. We used an ETF to invest in gold and we can also use an ETF to invest in gold miners.

The VanEck Vectors Gold Miners ETF (GDX) is designed to track the NYSE Arca Gold Miners Index and invests at least 80% of its holdings in companies that comprise the index. This provides exposure to both gold and silver miners. At the time of writing, the ETF pays a dividend that yields 0.52%, so there will be a small distribution to reinvest. At 0.52%, a $10,000 investment yields $52 per year. If you're looking to support yourself on dividend income, gold mining stocks aren't your best bet, but when used as a hedge, the small compounding effect provides an advantage that you won't get from a gold bullion ETF.

The U.S. Global GO GOLD and Precious Metal Miners ETF (GOAU) is, as the name implies, designed to track the performance of the U.S. Global GO Gold and Precious Metal

Miners Index. The index is comprised of common stocks or depository receipts that earn at least 50% of their aggregate revenue from precious metals. At the time writing, the ETF pays a dividend that yields 0.13%. So again, enjoy the small compounding effect that this provides, but don't quit your day job and expect to live sufficiently on the dividend income.

These aren't the only gold miners ETFs available. They're presented here because they are two of the larger funds, they're heavily traded, and therefore sufficiently liquid. Before investing in any market, it's important to conduct your own research and pick the fund that meets your investment objectives. Gold miners ETFs have an average expense ratio of 0.74%. The amount you pay to hold an investment should always be taken into consideration.

In addition to investing in gold miners, some investors make room in their portfolio for junior gold miners. A junior is analogous to a small cap company. Many of them are still in the exploratory phase and their potential profits are tied to whether or not they "strike gold." Naturally, a junior gold miners ETF is going to be more volatile than a senior gold miners ETF, just as a small cap stock index is going to be more volatile than the S&P 500. This is okay as long as you buy the ETF because you want the volatility. When it comes to the science of investing in gold, the decision to increase volatility should be made with respect to all of your holdings. It's not a factor of whether or not a highly volatile junior gold miners ETF is right for you, but a factor of how that ETF behaves relative to your other holdings. Exposure to volatility can provide a long-term benefit through rebalancing, but can also wreak havoc on short-term results. The key is to understand the volatility, how your different holdings interact, and what a reasonable long-term return is expected to look like.

Not all junior gold miners ETFs are built the same. The VanEck Vectors Junior Gold Miners ETF (GDXJ) states in their prospectus that the "index includes companies . . . that have mining projects with the potential to generate greater than 50% of their revenues from gold and/or silver when developed." The word "potential" gives the fund managers quite a bit of leeway when selecting stocks for inclusion. This doesn't mean that the VanEck Vectors Junior Gold Miners ETF (GDXJ) is a bad investment. Rather, it means investors should understand what they're investing in as they construct their portfolios.

So how exactly does the science of investing in gold miners ETFs work? It's just like the science of investing with gold. The ETF does not become our primary focus, but instead serves as a hedge. It limits our losses when other investments perform poorly, and the act of rebalancing facilitates a buy-low, sell-high mechanism that will improve total portfolio returns. Like before, we skim gains off the top of advancing asset classes in order to reinvest at a discount in asset classes that are bottoming.

I previously recommended a 5% to 10% allocation when using gold as a hedge. Should you decide to hedge with gold mining stocks instead of gold, this allocation can still be used. However, when you consider that gold miners function as a leveraged investment, similar results can be achieved with a smaller allocation. If we expect gold miners to advance by more than gold during a bull run and then retreat by more than gold during a bear market, cutting the allocation back to somewhere in the vicinity of 3% makes sense. You get the job done with a smaller allocation, which enables you to invest even more in asset classes that pay a distribution.

The following chart compares the GDX (gold miners) to the GLD (gold bullion) over the five-year period stretching from June 2015 through June 2020. The Dow Jones Industrial Average is also included for comparative purposes.

GDX vs GLD: June 2015 thru June 2020

As expected, the gold miners index is more volatile than gold. When the spot price of gold increases, the GDX goes up by more than the GLD. When the spot price of gold falls, the GDX goes down by more than the GLD. By early 2017, the GDX has doubled in value. In early 2020, it falls back below the GLD. Then they both take off. The GDX, of course, gains more ground. At one point, the gain exceeds 200%. That's impressive when you consider that an investment in the Dow Jones Industrial Average or S&P 500 will, on average, double every ten years. Gold has the propensity to get the job done faster, and gold miners stocks have the propensity to get the job done several times over. When investing in gold as an art, it's a matter of timing. When investing in gold as a science, it's a matter of letting your asset classes work through their cycles.

There will be times when greater volatility leads to larger gains and protection against a falling stock market. There will be other times when volatility leads to sharp declines. Whether this is good or bad depends largely on your investment horizon. Referring again to the above chart, think about rebalancing between the GLD and the Dow compared to rebalancing between the GDX and the Dow. We've already discussed the merits of rebalancing based on the Dow/gold ratio and how this approach can be used to combine both the art and science of investing in gold. We also understand how gold behaves as a portfolio hedge. If, instead of hedging with gold, we hedge with gold mining stocks, the long-term benefits and short-term setbacks are amplified. In the short-term, this can be either good or bad, depending on which direction gold moves. In the long-term it's good because all of your asset classes will move through multiple cycles; the broad movements of the gold mining ETF means that you recognize larger gains and buy deeper discounts than you would with gold.

If you also invest in silver, it should be noted that very few companies mine exclusively for silver. You might invest in both gold bullion and silver bullion ETFs, but the mining ETFs are different. A gold mining ETF is going to include companies that mine both gold and silver, so your exposure to these commodities is combined.

A final word on using gold as a portfolio hedge: the choice between gold and gold mining ETFs is not mutually exclusive (both can be added to the portfolio). It's important to understand the risk that each entails. If you currently allocate 10% of your portfolio to gold, the decision to add a gold mining ETF likely means that you should reduce your exposure to gold. Say you want to allocate 3% of the portfolio to gold miners, then exposure to your gold ETF should be reduced to at least 7% (or even lower, considering that the gold mining ETFs functions as a leveraged investment).

The Art of Investing in Gold Mining Stocks

Now we're going to focus on everything that this book isn't supposed to be about—*we're going to pick individual stocks*. The art of stock selection is as challenging as the art of gold investing. When the two are combined, large gains can be recognized at specific points in the economic cycle. When the timing isn't right or the company turns out to be more mismanaged than anyone could have possibly realized, losses ensue. Like gold, gold mining stocks outperform at specific points in the economic cycle; they also behave like complete duds at other points. These are stocks, but they aren't strongly correlated with the greater stock market. During the Great Depression, stocks tanked, but gold mining stocks proved to be one of the best investments of the era. Should we ever experience another depression, gold mining stocks might be the way to go.

The art of stock selection is beyond the scope of a single chapter. It can't be thoroughly covered in a single book. Successful investors read a lot. They learn a lot, too. The investors who remain successful are the ones that never stop learning. In my previous releases, *Dividend Investing*, *Preparing For Financial Success*, and *Beating The Market*, ample space is dedicated to stock selection. I won't repeat the material here. Instead, I'm going to focus on attributes that are most applicable to gold mining stocks. This includes AISC, the current ratio, the debt-to-equity ratio, foreign currency exposure, and dividend yield.

One advantage of gold mining stocks over gold is that you can calculate their intrinsic value . . . *at least in theory*. We're dealing with companies now, which means we can make estimates about future earnings. Some of these companies pay a small dividend, so we can also make estimates about future distributions. Then we discount our estimates back to present value and add them all up. *Voila!* We have intrinsic value. The only problem is that in order to estimate future earnings and the capacity to pay future dividends, we have to estimate what the spot price of gold is going to be each year for the next several decades. It's incredibly difficult to predict the future price of a commodity that doesn't increase in line with the average rate of inflation. In other words, the effort we might dedicate to calculating the intrinsic value of a gold mining company can be put to better use elsewhere. Beyond my willingness to speculate on short-term trends, I have no idea what the spot price of gold will be at any point in the future. Your guess is as good as mine.

Instead of focusing on intrinsic value, we're going to focus on efficiency. Does the company have a history of keeping costs under control? This is an area where the seniors have significantly more data to judge from than the juniors. In all honesty, I mostly avoid the juniors. There are times when I assume modest exposure through an ETF, but investing in the individual stocks is risky business. I prefer gold miners with a long history of efficiency. There's a survivorship bias at play, and the bias works to our advantage. Gold mining is competitive. If a company lacks basic efficiencies, they won't survive, which means they'll cease to be an investment option. The benefit of the seniors is that we know they survived. They already have a vote in their favor. A year-over-year expense comparison is the first step. How much does it cost them versus the competition to mine an ounce of gold? Past performance is never a guarantee of future performance, but all else being equal, the company with the longest history of comparatively efficient operations is your best bet. All else *not* being equal, the current environment, which includes the number and location of mines at their disposal, the age of their equipment, the amount of outstanding debt, and the strength of their labor relations, all come into play. A company with new mines can conceivably fare better than a company working from a longstanding mine. The deeper you have to dig in order to locate more gold, the more expensive the extraction. A new mine provides an opportunity for cheap extraction, assuming the mine holds as much gold as expected.

A lot of gold mining companies go out of business during a prolonged bear market. The ones that persevere do so because they're tightly managed. There's a reason why Warren Buffett picked Barrick Gold Corporation (GOLD) when he turned bullish on gold. They have a history of efficiency. If your goal is to acquire a successful gold mining stock just in time for the next bull run, this is the type of company you should consider.

Gold mining is a capital-intensive industry. There are high barriers to entry. This provides protection to those with a proven track record of efficiency. It's entirely possible that an underdog will step up to the plate and knock one out of the park, but given that gold mining stocks already function as a leveraged investment, searching for the next Starbucks Corporation (SBUX) of the industry isn't just risky, it's unnecessary. The art of investing in gold mining stocks already entails sufficient risk and the potential for a correspondingly high reward. You can take it further if you want, but we're already playing a high stakes game, so I really don't see the point in adding more greed to the equation.

All In Sustaining Costs (AISC)

The most important metric in this industry is All In Sustaining Costs (AISC). It measures all direct and recurring costs required to mine a unit of ore. Each miner will incur a different level of cost to both extract and refine the gold, yet the price that gold can be sold for is relatively uniform across companies. It's the company with the lowest AISC that's going to earn the largest return per ounce. Given that this is an industry where the selling price is the same for all companies, the ability to excavate, extract, and refine at a lower cost is the only way to outperform. The lower the AISC, the better.

Cash is king. That doesn't mean we don't care about net income, return on equity, P/E ratio, and all those other attributes we use to evaluate stocks. But positive cash flow is what keeps the gold miners alive. If they don't keep costs under control, their cash flow suffers. They can improve cash flow by becoming more efficient, but once this is achieved, the only way to recognize further improvements in cash flow is for the spot price of gold to go up. That's all there is to it. If they're managed efficiently, it means their costs are "fixed." When the amount that they can earn from their extractions goes up, they suddenly have more cash at their disposal. Another way of saying this is that an increase in the spot price of gold leads to an increase in margin. Net income resultantly goes up, as does return on equity. An older company that has persevered through several economic cycles and used these sporadic increases in cash flow to reduce their debt position will maintain a lower AISC moving forward. That's why I recommend investing in the seniors. They've had amplc opportunity to chisel away at their debt. This creates a financial efficiency that's carried forward in perpetuity.

Current Ratio

This next attribute might surprise you, but I always scrutinize the current ratio when evaluating gold miners. The current ratio is calculated by taking current assets over current liabilities:

$$\text{Current Ratio} = \text{Current Assets} / \text{Current Liabilities}$$

A ratio greater than 1 is a sign of stability. This means that the company isn't expected to face any disruptions in the normal course of business over the next year.

Most investors look for a current ratio greater than 1, but they're not going to buy a stock just because of the ratio. After all, an innovative technology company doesn't gain momentum because they have a large current ratio, but instead gains momentum when they successfully bring an innovative new product to market. A similar analogy can be made for most industries. A current ratio greater than 1 simply means that the company is in a position to carry on for at least the next year, but it doesn't really speak to how successful the company is.

When it comes to gold miners, a high current ratio holds greater meaning. Instead of just verifying that it's greater than 1, give extra consideration to companies with high ratios, say, somewhere around 2 or even higher. When the spot price of gold drops, companies with high current ratios fare better than those with low current ratios. A company that has built their ratio up to something higher than that of the competition did so by operating efficiently. Even if the spot price doesn't fall, these are the companies that outperform when the trend is up. When the trend is down, they still take a beating, but they're much less likely to close shop.

Debt

Debt isn't necessarily bad. Companies acquire debt in order to take on new projects. But too much debt can hold a company back, especially in an industry where efficiency is vital. It's important to not only look at a company's debt obligation, but to also compare the debt-to-equity ratio for each of the companies you're considering.

Debt-to-Equity Ratio = Debt / Equity

Each gold mining company takes on debt for the same reasons: to find gold, set up shop, and drill. The company that has accomplished this and then worked to reduce its debt is in a better position than the company still striving to reduce its debt. Typically, the smaller the debt-to-equity ratio, the better. A larger debt position could coincide with the acquisition of a new mine, but the company that has reduced their debt and still has plenty of gold left to mine is in a better position.

Foreign Currency Exposure

Gold mining companies are spread across the globe. These are international investments that provide exposure to foreign markets, but the exposure is very concentrated. Your return is based primarily on efficiency and the spot price of gold. Don't confuse an investment in a gold mining company that owns mines in developing parts of the world for an emerging market play. Your return is correlated with the spot price of gold, not the economic vigilance of emerging markets.

It goes without saying that when you invest in gold mining companies, you don't need to be as heavily exposed to bullion. The gold mining company provides this exposure for you. But there's one more bird that gets killed with that same stone. Regardless of where you live or your tolerance for risk, at least part of your portfolio should be allocated to foreign markets. Foreign investments not only provide exposure to foreign economies, they also provide exposure to foreign currencies. This is important from a diversification perspective. At least a portion of the portfolio should provide global exposure. Even more important is that the global exposure shouldn't be too heavily concentrated in a single region. Perhaps you'll invest in bonds from the Asia Pacific, stocks from EMEA, and REITs in Canada. Or maybe you'll take a completely different approach. Whatever the case, there's now a global impact when you rebalance your portfolio, and foreign currency valuation is a part of that impact. This provides protection against a weakening U.S. dollar, but it does so in a way that negates the risk of simply parking your money in the fiat currency of a foreign country. Yes, all of the foreign currencies you're now exposed to will decline in value as the respective governments print more, but you're also invested in income generating assets. In other words, your foreign currency exposure should be in the form of an inflation hedge, not purely in the form of a currency.

Foreign currency exposure makes a difference. Now we're not simply rebalancing between funds that generated different amounts of revenue, but also rebalancing across funds denominated in currencies that strengthen and weaken against each other, many of which strengthen and weaken in alternating intervals.

When you invest in an ETF that tracks gold mining companies, the notion of reducing your exposure to bullion is obvious, but there's a more subtle exposure that's easily overlooked in this situation, and that's your exposure to foreign currencies. If you're holding foreign stocks to gain exposure to specific regions that you might be bullish on, your exposure to gold miners is unlikely to overlap with these investments. But if a portion of your bond allocation is spread across the globe in an effort to gain foreign currency exposure, you now have some overlap.

When it comes to bullion, it's recommended that you decrease your bullion exposure by more than the respective allocation to gold mining companies because the gold miners function as a leveraged investment in gold. Gold mining companies do not, however, operate as a leveraged investment in foreign currency. Instead, they provide exposure to specific currencies. A modest allocation to gold miners that operate in foreign countries should be met with an equally modest, or perhaps even less modest, reduction in your foreign currency exposure. The key is to understand what you're exposed to.

Dividend Yield

With gold miners, the question of whether to distribute a dividend or reinvest the proceeds is less important than for companies in innovative sectors. When it comes to the technology sector, investors often forgo dividend-payers because they believe that the prospect for growth is better when companies reinvest their earnings in innovative new projects. This does not apply to gold miners. Innovations in the extraction process are more likely to come from the companies that sell equipment to gold miners, rather than directly from the mining companies. A dividend distribution, no matter how small, should be viewed as a sign of strength. Even if the distribution is negligible compared to that of a dividend aristocrat like 3M Company (MMM) or Colgate-Palmolive Company (CL), a gold mining stock that pays a small dividend has strength. It just might be the efficient company you've been searching for.

When to buy?

The information we discussed so far will assist you in deciding which gold mining company(s) to invest in, but the question on the tip of your tongue is, *when do I buy?* In Chapter 7, we discussed economic indicators that are commonly followed by gold investors. When it comes to gold mining stocks, there's no need to reinvent the wheel. A bullish indicator for gold is also a bullish indicator for gold miners. There is, however, a notable advantage with gold miners; the spot price of gold is also an extremely useful economic indicator. If the spot price of gold goes up and the gold miners have yet to follow, then it's time to buy gold mining stocks. If gold continues to outpace the gold miners, then it's time to average up and buy more. Eventually, the gold miners will follow suit. When the benefit of leverage kicks in, they will quickly outpace the upward trend in gold.

It really doesn't get any easier than that. When gold advances ahead of the gold miners, it's the golden opportunity you've been waiting for. This is one of the strongest indicators that you'll ever see for a leveraged investment. The only downside is that it doesn't happen very often. It might happen next week or it could take a few years. Maybe five. Or a decade could slip by before the next really strong gold miners stock indicator starts flashing. That's what makes it an art. You watch, you wait, and when it happens, you pounce. Then you need to get out before it's over. Like before, moving in shifts is advised. Once you have a nice gain, take a little back, and then keep taking more as the market (*hopefully*) trends higher. After you close the position, it's time to invest in something else until gold once again advances ahead of the gold miners. It could be several years or longer. Or, depending on fiscal policy and the state of the economy, it's possible that you'll catch two runs back-to-back in short successions. Consider it luck if you do.

A long-term look

The World Gold Council estimates that there are 54,000 tons of extractable gold buried beneath the earth. At the current rate of extraction, there's a good chance that all 54,000 tons will be mined within the next 20 years. This poses an interesting conundrum for those who invest in gold mining stocks. Historically, these companies have been positively correlated with the spot price of gold. Once all the gold that we know of has been extracted, one can only imagine that the gold mining companies will have to focus on other metals. The stocks, conceivably, will go down in price, while the spot price of gold will conceivably go up.

Naturally, a lot will unfold between now and then. More gold could be discovered. Even if it's not, we shouldn't expect all of the gold mining companies to be impacted equally. Some mines will be depleted quicker than others. Those with the most exposure to fully functioning mines could continue in full operation while competing companies close shop or redirect their efforts to silver, copper, iron ore, or even lead. In other words, it's not just that the gold mining companies have the potential to break their correlation with the spot price of bullion, they also have the potential to break correlation with each other.

It's too early to implement a strategy to time the potential disruption of this industry. But it's definitely something to keep an eye on over the next couple of decades.

Chapter 10: Digital Gold

Can gold be digitized? This might have been a foolish question in the past, but today the answer appears to be, *Yes!* In late 2017, there was a gold rush of sorts in the cryptocurrency market as Bitcoin went through the roof. Investors had an opportunity to become disgustingly rich, provided they got out before the market crashed. Almost overnight, a highly speculative digital currency that had been trading for pennies rocketed all the way to $19,800 per unit. As is generally the case when mass hysteria pushes an asset to extraordinary levels, the party didn't last long. By January 2018, it looked like Bitcoin was more akin to digital tulip bulbs than to digital gold. In the months following the rise, it fell from $19,800 to $3,200. The rise and fall is very reminiscent of tulip mania, except for one notable difference: Bitcoin keeps coming back. It's like one of those *Friday the 13th* movies where you keep thinking that Jason Vorhees has finally died, but alas, he comes back again . . . and again . . . and again.

All joking aside, the ups and downs of Bitcoin have been frightening. There was another bull run in the first half of 2019, followed by a slower and more gradual bear trend that gave way to a number of fake comebacks along the way. Bitcoin has a lot in common with Jason Vorhees. It's the asset class that doesn't die, it has a cult following, and there are plenty of proponents who want the comebacks to be real. The role of the cryptocurrency is still being defined, as is the extent to which the investment community is willing to embrace cryptocurrencies.

The purpose of this chapter isn't to debate the merits of cryptocurrencies. I won't be making predictions about where the cryptocurrency market or specific cryptocurrencies are headed. Instead, I'm going to discuss the similarities and differences between cryptocurrencies and gold. We'll also discuss strategies that can be used as a side bet.

Some investors believe that the cryptocurrency market will make them rich. Others won't touch these "currencies" with a ten-foot pole. I believe that there's room in the portfolio for cryptocurrencies if the investor not only understands the risk, but is also willing to accept the risk. Just like with physical gold, there's both an art and a science to investing in digital gold. The asset allocator might allocate as much as 10% of their portfolio to gold because it's a strong defensive asset that has been sought after for well over 5,000 years. Cryptocurrencies, on the other hand, have ten years of history, are highly volatile, and are still fighting for acceptance as a medium of exchange. There is potential for large returns. There is also potential for large losses. The asset allocator that is willing to accept this risk might want to limit their exposure to 5% (or maybe 2.5%, just to play it safe). Those who practice the art of investing in cryptocurrencies are advised to only invest what they can afford to lose. Remember, just because it came back from the dead before doesn't mean it will do so again. They stopped making *Friday the 13th* movies back in 2003, and efforts to reboot the franchise in 2009 were short-lived.

Blockchain Technology

Even if you don't invest in cryptocurrencies, it's likely that you're familiar with the term blockchain. It's important to understand that blockchain and cryptocurrencies are not one in the same. In essence, blockchain is the ledger on which cryptocurrencies are exchanged. It's a decentralized peer-to-peer network that's completely transparent. Your bank, for example, stores all of its transactions on a private ledger. You can see your account and your transactions, but you can't see the entire ledger. It's not transparent. Instead, it's subject to audit in order to provide assurance that the bank follows regulations and is in a position to make good on your deposits. With blockchain, there's no central location. It's a network that everyone has access to. The transactions are anonymous but visible. This increases accuracy and reduces fraud. It also makes it difficult to correct mistakes.

Bitcoin, Ethereum, Litecoin, and Ripple are all cryptocurrencies that are exchanged on a blockchain. The question that many investors struggle with is, should I invest in cryptocurrencies or in companies that develop blockchain technology? To a certain extent, the question is similar to, should I invest in gold or gold mining companies? The primary difference is that most blockchain developers produce and provide other technology related products and services. There aren't any blue-chip companies dedicated solely to the development of blockchain technology. However, startups that focus on blockchain technology are not in short supply. My advice is to research these companies thoroughly before making an investment. A blue-chip company provides greater safety because their product line isn't limited to blockchain technology. At the same time, they can't provide much in terms of growth. The momentum in the technology sector and the increasing number of startups is eerily reminiscent of the dot-com bubble. It would be foolish to invest in a startup simply because they develop blockchain technology. But if the company has been thoroughly researched and the outlook is promising, an investment that's in line with your tolerance for risk may be warranted.

The use of blockchain technology extends beyond cryptocurrencies. Blockchains can also be used to store medical records, insurance policies, property deeds, automobile titles, and voting records. The possibilities are limitless. Bullish blockchain investors believe that this technology will catch on and replace many of the systems currently in place. The growing acceptance of cryptocurrencies is thought to be just the tip of the iceberg.

My advice is to make room in the portfolio for both cryptocurrencies and companies that develop blockchain technology. Cryptocurrencies are highly volatile and speculative and should therefore receive a modest allocation. Companies that develop blockchain technology have the potential to deliver large returns, but it's unlikely that they'll provide the quick and voracious returns that the winners of the crypto race are expected to provide. It's more of a buy-and-hold strategy.

You can invest directly in companies that are leading the blockchain innovation or you can buy a sector ETF. An ETF that tracks the technology sector will provide exposure to companies that offer a broad array of technology driven products and services. By investing in a technology sector ETF, you'll receive modest exposure to blockchain technology. If you opt for an ETF that only invests in companies that are involved in the development of blockchain technology, you'll get more exposure, but you still get exposure to different product lines. The Amplify Transformational Data Sharing ETF (BLOK) is an option that's gaining popularity. It has an average trading volume just shy of 1 million trades per day. At the time of writing, it's difficult to invest exclusively in blockchain technology, but it's easy to invest exclusively in the cryptocurrency of your choice.

When adding stocks and ETFs to your portfolio, be aware of any possible overlap between funds. If you already have exposure to the technology sector, you might be covered. If you want to increase your exposure to blockchain technology without increasing your exposure to the entire sector, you'll need to be mindful of which companies you already have exposure to.

Similarities with gold

We like gold because the government can't print more of it. The same applies to cryptocurrencies. I don't mean to suggest that *all* cryptocurrencies are finite in quantity and will never be expanded upon. Many of them do provide scarcity, but it's not a prerequisite. Bitcoin, for example, is limited to 21,000,000 units. The overarching allure is that governments don't control cryptocurrencies (unless they create their own). They can't print more Bitcoin and the stakeholders have a vested interest in protecting the scarcity of their currency. In this regard, cryptocurrencies are viewed as having a unique type of protection over fiat currencies, even if other vulnerabilities are possible. Ethereum, for example, isn't manipulated by the government in an effort to stimulate the economy and curb unemployment. Instead, the creators of Ethereum are concerned with the value and usefulness of Ethereum. The creators of Litecoin are similarly concerned with the value and usefulness of Litecoin. The list goes on. One of the many advantages to cryptocurrencies is that they serve as a global medium of exchange that is disjointed from the political agenda of governments. In this regard, cryptocurrencies are like gold, at least in their current state. Governments around the world are starting to develop their own cryptocurrencies, just as they developed their own fiat currencies. This can be viewed as a bullish sign for cryptocurrencies. They're gaining global acceptance, not just from the prophets of doom and gloom who bury gold in their back yards, but from governments, businesses, and financial institutions. This is a bullish sign, but the question of scarcity still remains. Which cryptocurrencies are the equivalent of digital gold? And which cryptocurrencies will become the equivalent of a digital fiat currency? The answer is a deciding factor for investors. We want the digital gold.

When you invest in cryptocurrencies, you're interacting with global participants. This means that there's a lack of regulation. It's the same with gold and, to a similar extent, with forex trading. If you log into your digital wallet one day and it's mysteriously empty, who do you turn to? There's no FDIC insurance for cryptocurrencies. While it's common practice to insure gold, an insurance market for cryptocurrencies doesn't yet exist. When you leave the safety of a regulated exchange, the potential for fraud increases. Holding cryptocurrencies in an ETF provides a certain degree of protection. Let the experts buy and sell the cryptocurrencies while you invest in their fund by way of a regulated exchange, just as you would with a gold ETF.

Like gold, cryptocurrencies are not income producing assets. They don't earn interest, pay dividends, or generate wealth. You buy them, hold them, and then either sell them or exchange them for goods. That's it. Their value isn't derived from usefulness, but instead, derived from the public's acceptance that they hold value.

The Bitcoin bubble of 2017 was the second largest bubble in history, just behind tulip mania. It was bigger than the South Sea Company bubble, the Dow Jones bubble of 1929, the Nikkei bubble of 1989, and the housing crisis of 2007-2008.

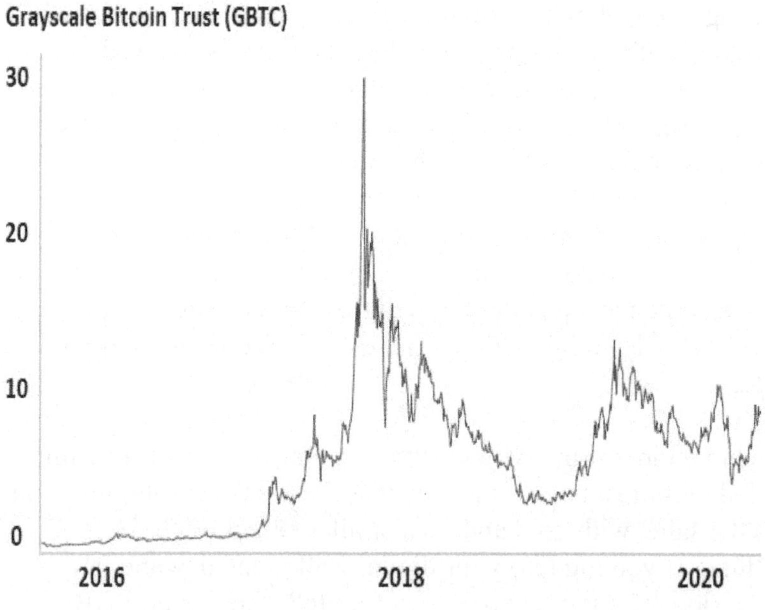

While gold has yet to set a record in the bubble department, it's still susceptible to mass hysteria. After the Bretton Woods agreement was abandoned in 1971, gold went through the roof. The bull market lasted until 1980, at which point it traversed into a nasty bear market that lasted for 26 years. The bull market for gold lasted longer than the bull market for Bitcoin, but they both endured a similar, albeit temporary, crash. Then volatility set in. Gold moved sideways for a prolonged period of time while exhibiting up and down schizophrenic tendencies. The behavior of Bitcoin has also been schizophrenic, but we have yet to see where the long-term trend will take us.

The volatility of cryptocurrencies lends itself to trading. Trading is a highly speculative endeavor that exposes participants to the opportunity to recognize large gains and losses. This is different from the art of investing in gold, yet at the same time it's perplexingly similar. Gold is only a long-term buy-and-hold asset when used as a portfolio hedge. The gold investor can then increase their exposure when fear, inflation, and economic uncertainty are on the horizon. A similar trend is emerging with cryptocurrencies, but we don't have enough historical data to make meaningful conjectures on what the results are going to be. It's too soon to label any cryptocurrencies as a store of value. The similarities between gold and cryptocurrencies have led some investors to treat cryptocurrencies as such anyways. This trend has yet to conform to the price movements of gold because the cryptocurrency investors are butting heads with the cryptocurrency traders, all while the cryptocurrency consumer remains underrepresented. How these conflicting positions will be resolved in the long run is a matter of speculation. Should consumer adoption of cryptocurrencies increase, it's possible that the price will undergo stabilization. The traders could conceivably get squeezed out, allowing cryptocurrencies to truly serve as a store of value. This, of course, is simply a projection, and determining which cryptocurrencies will survive to become the store of value is another question altogether.

In Chapter 7, we discussed how gold competes with bonds for the "non-equity" component of the portfolio. Bonds are likely to win when interest rates are attractive, while gold only receives a fighting chance when interest rates are slashed in an effort to spur economic activity. Cryptocurrencies have now taken a seat at the table, but they aren't going to beat bonds on interest rates. Like gold, the yield is zero.

Some might argue that cryptocurrencies aren't just fighting for a seat at the table, but have in fact increased the size of the table. The Millennials have been slow to embrace traditional methods of investing, but they've come to understand cryptocurrencies quite well, and what cryptocurrencies have taught them is that traditional fiat currencies that are subject to mass printing decline in value. It's not just investors who need protection, but savers and consumers too. The economics of a cryptocurrency that's fixed in quantity is similar to that of a precious metal that's also fixed in quantity. As a result, Millennials are now starting to embrace gold and silver. Demand has increased while supply remains fixed, which is just one of many bullish factors that has pushed gold higher.

Moving forward, it's possible that cryptocurrencies will correlate with gold, maintaining value as the dollar weakens, and falling in price when the dollar strengthens. It's also possible that cryptocurrencies will exhibit higher volatility, gaining more than gold during times of uncertainty and losing more than gold during times of prosperity. Twenty years from now, if there really is no more gold left to mine, cryptocurrencies could easily replace gold mining stocks as a leveraged alternative to gold. Or they could do something completely different. At this point, we simply don't know.

Differences from gold

The biggest difference between cryptocurrencies and gold is volatility. Sure, both asset classes can be used to hedge the shortcomings of a fiat currency, but the speculative nature of cryptocurrencies leads to erratic behavior. We've already seen what happened during the Bitcoin bubble. To call the behavior erratic is an understatement. Let's ignore the bubble and focus on how Bitcoin behaved after the investing public had time to digest the mass hysteria. Between January 2019 and March 2020, both Bitcoin and gold outperformed the S&P 500. Bitcoin beat it by a lot more, but took the investor on a wild ride in the process.

When it comes to the art of investing, the more predictable the behavior, the easier it is to master. Cryptocurrencies are challenging because they lack predictability. Whether this should be seen as an opportunity or an obstacle depends on the strategy you implement. I view it as an obstacle. Even when applying the science of investing to cryptocurrencies, I only give digital currencies a tiny allocation, nothing greater than 2.5%.

The demand for gold stems from the fact that it's available to many different types of investors, not just speculators. While this book isn't focused on the investor who buys physical gold in preparation for a financial system collapse, this investor exists nonetheless, and their buying habits factor into the demand for gold. No such investor exists for cryptocurrencies. It's impossible for the cryptocurrency investor to take physical possession. Vaulting services are starting to add cryptocurrency platforms to their array of services, but it's going to be stored on a blockchain, not in a vault. There's nothing for the prophets of doom and gloom to bury in their back yards. In this regard, cryptocurrencies provide the possibility of protection against inflation and the overprinting of fiat currencies—and it can even be argued that they provide protection against a bank holiday, given that the blockchain is decentralized and transparent—but they do not provide protection against complete financial Armageddon. Should we ever revert to the ways of our primitive past, bullion will provide protection that isn't available from a digital asset. I'm not overly concerned with the prospect of this happening, and I'm still inclined to believe that cans of beans, or even coffee, will be the ultimate form of currency under such conditions.

Let's not be pessimists. An investment strategy should be geared towards making money, not towards protecting ourselves against the unlikely collapse of our financial infrastructure. Cryptocurrencies have the potential to function like gold, even if there's no such thing as taking physical possession. The fact that you can't take possession can actually be viewed as a benefit. There's no storage cost, no insurance companies to deal with, and there's no risk of burglars breaking into your home. These are huge advantages. Yes, we sacrifice the feeling of security that comes with holding a bar of bullion. There's no true glitter, just the simulation of glitter on our computer screen. But when we forfeit these cosmetic properties, we lower the cost of investing and increase the ease of transacting.

Will a cryptocurrency ever usurp gold's role as the default currency? Will the world leaders someday agree to fall back on Bitcoin in the event that all fiat currencies fail? I don't expect such an agreement to appear in tomorrow's headlines, but at the rate technology is moving, it could be closer than we realize. What this would do to the price of gold is a matter of speculation. I don't have the answer. But if you feel more comfortable with physical assets, I recommend adding real estate to the portfolio. The use of gold as money can be simulated and even replaced with digital assets. All it takes is widespread acceptance. Perhaps easier said than done, but possible nonetheless. A roof over someone's head cannot be simulated with a digital asset. Those who bury gold in their back yard may one day wish that they'd opted for making a down payment on the house next door instead.

Signs of acceptance

Investors are turning to cryptocurrencies as an alternative asset, but it's important to remember that these currencies will only increase in value if consumer acceptance follows. If people don't transact with Bitcoin, then it will become worthless to both consumers and investors alike. There are two important questions that investors should ask before investing in a specific coin: Does the coin have value and solve problems that aren't addressed by fiat currencies? Do consumers—not fellow investors, but consumers also see the value that this coin creates?

Whether you've been following cryptocurrencies or not, you've heard the buzzwords. For some, they're a source of curiosity. For others, it's a means to take the control of money away from governments and large corporations and put it in the hands of ordinary people. Cryptocurrencies are gaining ground, but the day when cryptocurrencies will be accepted everywhere feels like it exists only in the distant future. A lot of big companies have yet to embrace digital currencies, which creates an opportunity for their competition to gain a competitive advantage. In Europe, the smaller food delivery services are starting to accept Bitcoin, yet the larger service providers are hesitant to adapt. If you want to use Bitcoin to pay for delivery from Uber Eats, you can, but Uber Eats won't accept your payment directly. Instead, you have to go through an intermediary that specializes in placing orders on behalf of consumers. In the U.S., there aren't very many delivery services that accept Bitcoin, but we can place an order through PizzaForCoins and let them order the pizza.

Websites that list businesses willing to accept Bitcoin and similar currencies are popping up all over the Internet. You can look for a website dedicated to your city or wherever you might be traveling. Speaking of traveling, airBaltic from Latvia is the world's first national airline to accept Bitcoin. Most major hotels and airlines have yet to embrace cryptocurrencies, but if this changes, the impact will be tremendous. Given that these are global currencies, acceptance within the travel industry would be incredibly bullish.

It's not surprising that the overwhelming majority of companies accepting cryptocurrencies have an online presence. Some of them conduct business exclusively online. If you do business with Microsoft, they'll accept payment in Bitcoin. Wikipedia accepts donations in Bitcoin. If you're in the dating market, OKCupid now accepts payment in Bitcoin. If you partake in online gambling (not advised), there are plenty of websites willing to accept cryptocurrencies in exchange for showering you with flashing lights (and a chance, I suppose, at winning that jackpot). Other cryptocurrencies, like Ethereum and Litecoin, are gaining acceptance from online retailers, but they have yet to make a real impact with brick and mortar businesses—*at least for now.* Depending on where you live, a Bitcoin ATM might be a regular fixture at the mall. Should Ethereum, Litecoin, or any other cryptocurrency follow suit, it could be the bullish signal that investors are waiting for.

What about bonds denominated in cryptocurrencies that pay interest in said currency? This would be interesting. Not only would it be bullish for cryptocurrencies as a medium of exchange, but also as a store of value.

Investors are clearly backing Bitcoin. In the first half of 2020, Bitcoin outperformed both the S&P 500 and the Nasdaq, but it did so with an immense amount of volatility. If an investor got in during a peak rather than a valley, they lost money. The slow and steady returns that make a prolonged bull market easy to play have yet to be found in the cryptocurrency market. In order for volatility to diminish, acceptance from consumers needs to keep growing. Otherwise, the cryptocurrency investor will eventually come to find that they'd have been better off burying gold in their back yard.

The largest cohort of Bitcoin backers comes from the Millennial generation. They grew up tech savvy. They know nothing of a world without the Internet. When it comes to digital assets, they understand the value that a properly developed and sufficiently backed currency can provide. It was cryptocurrencies that taught Millennials about the benefit of scarcity and the dangers of a fiat currency. This, in turn, led the most technologically savvy generation to date to embrace the oldest form of money that we have—*gold!* It's about scarcity, and they get that. The big question is, are central banks going to embrace cryptocurrencies? The Millennials can buy all the digital gold they want, but the buying and selling of central banks would have an even bigger impact on the market. As cryptocurrencies continue to gain momentum, investors should keep an eye on the actions of central banks.

How to invest?

Discussions of how to invest in cryptocurrencies and how to both avoid scams and ensure that your investments are safe go hand-in-hand. There are investors who have lost thousands of dollars because they lost their password. Others have had their wallets hacked and their holdings liquidated. When investing in a global market that suffers from a lack of regulation, finding a secure method to make and store your investments is paramount. It doesn't matter how carefully you strategize your entry and exit points if you ultimately lose access to your holdings.

The most common medium of investing in cryptocurrencies is through a wallet, which is a digital means of storage. Various online platforms function as an exchange for trading the cryptocurrencies in your wallet. Most exchanges will permit you to fund your wallet via credit card, and from there you're off to the races. In many ways, the cryptocurrency marketplace is like the Wild Wild West. Fraud is prevalent and exchanges that provide protection in this poorly regulated environment are in demand. I'm not going to advocate any specific exchanges from a security perspective, but I can say that Coinbase, Bitfinex, Binance, and Robinhood are all popular exchanges.

If your goal is to build wealth by mastering the art of investing in cryptocurrencies, a digital currency exchange such as Coinbase might be the way to go. Many vaulting services now offer cryptocurrency trading as a service. If you have a longstanding relationship with the vault you hold your gold with, you might feel more comfortable working with them as you dive into the world of cryptocurrencies. Or you might decide to diversify your investments across different providers and keep your gold and cryptocurrencies separate, just in case one of the providers turns out to be pulling a Madoff. I can't make this decision for you. What I can do is show you a way to go against the grain, just as I have with my side bet, and make sure you understand the advantages and disadvantages of this approach.

If the world of digital currencies feels overly complex, an ETF that holds cryptocurrencies in trust can be purchased with the same ease as any other ETF. You'll pay a small fee, but that's about it. At the time of writing, your choices are limited. Not every cryptocurrency is tracked by an ETF. Just like with stocks, you can buy an ETF that represents the greater market, but it might not hold the currencies in the exact proportions that you desire. On top of that, given that this is both a volatile and emerging market, it's not uncommon for a cryptocurrency ETF to trade at a price that differs from the price of its holdings. For this reason, those looking to master the art of investing in cryptocurrencies are better off dealing directly with an exchange. Those who want to rely on the science of investing in cryptocurrencies might prefer the convenience of an ETF. Just like a gold ETF, it can be held in your stock portfolio alongside all of your other ETFs. This is exceptionally convenient when rebalancing the portfolio.

I know what you're thinking. I'm harking on the ease of transacting through an ETF, but your mind is still stuck on my statement that "it's not uncommon for a cryptocurrency ETF to trade at a price that differs from that of its holdings." Yes, this statement goes against the very ethos that successful investors subscribe to. You could overpay for the ETF and there's no guarantee that you'll get a fair price when it's time to get out of the ETF. It sounds risky. That's because it is. And it's not just the cryptocurrency ETF that's risky, it's cryptocurrencies in general. The market is still being established. The winners have yet to be identified. There's very little historic data to analyze. Volatility is rampant. Ethereum might be up 5% one day and down 10% the next. Even if today's price for an Ethereum ETF differs from today's price for Ethereum, who's to say that either one of them is priced fairly.

There are two reasons why an asset allocator might add a cryptocurrency ETF to their portfolio: (1) they think cryptocurrencies have a future and will provide strong long-term gains, and (2) they like the impact that the volatility has on their portfolio. Until the cryptocurrency market either matures or disappears, there's going to be a lot of volatility. These ETFs have been bouncing all over the place, and the act of rebalancing facilitates the buy-low, sell-high mechanism that we desire from a rebalancing strategy. If your Bitcoin ETF has fallen 15% since the last time you rebalanced, you'll systematically sell your outperforming assets in order to reinvest in Bitcoin. If the ETF is up 22% the next time you rebalance, you're going to sell some Bitcoin and put the proceeds back into your other asset classes. That's the beauty of adding a highly volatile asset class to your portfolio. As long as it's done in modest proportions, you should be able to stomach the ups and downs as you rebalance your way to a bigger portfolio. But I caution, keep the allocation small. With an accepted hedge like gold, we limit our exposure to 10%. With a highly volatile asset class that's still in its infancy, I recommend that those with a high tolerance for risk limit their exposure to 5%. If you have a low tolerance for risk, there's nothing wrong with forgoing cryptocurrencies altogether. There's a chance that Bitcoin will one day be completely worthless. All those years of volatility may have helped you increase the size of your portfolio, but you'll give it all back and then some if an entire piece of the pie goes belly up. We can diversify away the probability of Bitcoin becoming completely worthless the same way that we diversify away the probability of an individual stock becoming completely worthless. Instead of investing in an ETF that only holds Bitcoin, we invest in an ETF that provides broad exposure to the cryptocurrency market. Now the risk is reduced. This is still a volatile portfolio allocation, but we're protected from the probability of specific cryptocurrencies becoming obsolete. Our investment won't become worthless unless the entire cryptocurrency market becomes worthless. *How likely do you consider the prospect of that happening?* If you're worried, reread the signs of acceptance section above. Yes, it's possible. *But . . .*

Grayscale is currently leading the pack in terms of cryptocurrency ETFs, but it's likely that strong competition will emerge as cryptocurrencies continue to gain acceptance. Investment options include the following:

Grayscale Bitcoin Trust (GBTC)

Grayscale Ethereum Classic Trust (ETCG)

Grayscale Digital Large Cap Fund LLC (GDLC)

The first two selections provide exposure to Bitcoin and Ethereum, respectively. The Grayscale Digital Large Cap Fund LLC (GDLC) holds large cap digital assets that collectively comprise 70% of the entire digital currency market. The fund provides a convenient way to add cryptocurrencies to a fully diversified portfolio.

More on Strategy

I'm a firm believer in understanding how an investment works before putting money on the line. While the world of cryptocurrencies might feel overly complex, the utility of these currencies is actually quite simple. It's digital gold. They serve as a medium of exchange in a digital environment that's distinct and separate from government-issued fiat currencies. In a nutshell, *that's it!* But each cryptocurrency is different. Many have unique attributes that were developed in order to distinguish them from the herd. The functionality of each cryptocurrency is disclosed in what is known as the whitepaper. It's basically a prospectus that the developers use to sell the cryptocurrency. You could read the whitepaper of each cryptocurrency if you wanted, but most investors turn to trusted media outlets that explain the advantages and disadvantages of different cryptocurrencies.

I'm not going to focus too much on the art of investing in cryptocurrencies. It's very similar to the art of investing in gold, but with nuances that will vary between each cryptocurrency. In a sense, the fact that each cryptocurrency is different makes investing in them akin to investing in gold coins. The word numismatic has yet to be extended to cryptocurrencies, but just like gold coins, investors aren't just buying digital gold, but a specific issue of digital gold. I'd rather focus on the science because at this point in the evaluation of cryptocurrencies, the science is fascinating.

As a portfolio hedge, we expect the behavior of cryptocurrencies to be at times similar to, and at other times more volatile than, gold. Cryptocurrencies may or may not show strong positive correlation with gold, but they're similar to gold in that they do not show strong positive correlation with stocks. That's why they're a useful hedge.

What about the investor who has some extra money to burn and is interested in making a side bet? This investor might not feel comfortable timing the cryptocurrency market, but they still want to get in on the action. They're going to do so with a small sum of money and see if they can use the volatility of cryptocurrencies to earn a nice return. Let me show you how I play the cryptocurrency market. Think of it as food for thought. This approach may or may not be right for you.

I'm confident that cryptocurrencies will remain volatile (at least over the short-term). It's conceivable that as cryptocurrencies gain acceptance, leaders will emerge and the gains will be impressive. The act of rebalancing between dissimilar asset classes facilitates a buy-low, sell-high mechanism. The act of reinvesting dividends facilitates a dollar cost averaging mechanism that grows the entire pot through initial reinvestment in the underperforming assets. Here's how I've combined these pieces of conventional wisdom into a strategy:

I've taken a sum of money I can afford to lose and allocated 20% each to five different ETFs:

Grayscale Ethereum Classic Trust (ETCG)

Grayscale Bitcoin Trust (GBTC)

Grayscale Digital Large Cap Fund LLC (GDLC)

iShares Preferred and Income Securities ETF (PFF)

Invesco S&P 500 High Dividend Low Volatility ETF (SPHD)

I rebalance once a month as I simultaneously reinvest the dividend income from PFF and SPHD. Normally, rebalancing every month would be excessive, but the cryptocurrency market is so volatile that it's necessary in order to make the most of the peaks and valleys.

Both PFF and SPHD are included in the strategy because of their low volatility. These are equity investments that are, of course, susceptible to the whims of a stock market crash, but under normal circumstances they predominantly move sideways while dispersing large dividend distributions. At the time of writing, PFF yields 5.72% and SPHD yields 5.62%.

The advantage of pairing low- and high-volatility assets against each other is that gains are skimmed from the cryptocurrency funds as they advance and then are held in low-volatility dividend funds until the cryptocurrency funds retreat. When this happens, rebalancing forces us to put the proceeds back into the cryptocurrency funds at a now much lower price. I'm not speculating that the cryptocurrency funds will take off. Rather, I'm speculating that they remain volatile. Through rebalancing, I systematically trade back and forth between the dividend funds and the cryptocurrency funds. It works because the funds aren't positively correlated. This is lucrative. Over time, the pot gets bigger, and so does the stream of dividend income. In the event that one or more of the cryptocurrency funds enters bubble territory, *even better!* I could then liquidate all of the funds for a huge gain. But even if I miss the chance to exit, the act of rebalancing will have enabled me to recognize gains along the way.

For this side bet, I'm weighted 60% in cryptocurrencies and 40% in dividend stocks. If this exceeds your tolerance for risk, substitutions can be made. A gold ETF can be used to replace one of the cryptocurrency ETFs. Or you might want to add another divided-payer. You could even add one that's more volatile than PFF and SPHD, like a REIT fund.

When making side bets, a large cryptocurrency allocation can be used to churn big gains from the volatility. This essentially combines both the art and science of investing in cryptocurrencies. This approach isn't recommended for your retirement account. This approach should be applied to money that you don't plan to lose, but ultimately could afford to lose. I again recommend allocating no more than 5% of your greater portfolio to cryptocurrencies. If you have a low tolerance for risk, cryptocurrencies should be avoided altogether.

Chapter 11: Is There a Downside?

We've spent a lot of time discussing the ways that wealth can be built by investing strategically in gold. You might be asking, are there any downsides? The answer is yes, there are plenty of downsides. When it comes to the art of investing in gold, timing is everything. Where a stock investor strives to time the periods of economic expansion, the gold investor struggles to time the spurts of economic contraction. Society is working in favor of the stock investor and against the gold investor. Policymakers work hard to extend the periods of economic expansion and contain the spurts of economic contraction. The results of their fiscal policies aren't always as intended, but the odds are still stacked in favor of the stock investor. Our elected officials want to see the balances in our 401(k)s grow, not just for the good of the people, but so we don't become a burden to the system. They do not, however, care to enact policies that favor those who have bet against the U.S. dollar, yet they do so indirectly as they continue to print more of their fiat currency.

So what can't gold do for us? This is an important question, because an investor who gets in on a security because she likes the upside potential, but hasn't taken the time to fully understand the risks, is setting herself up for failure.

The first thing that the gold naysayers will tell you is that it's not an income producing asset. This is true. Gold doesn't pay interest or dividends and it can't generate any form of rent. It just sits there. It costs money to store. It costs money to insure. Even if you invest through an ETF, the trust that takes physical possession of the gold has to incur these costs, which get passed down to shareholders through the management fee. In this regard, gold is more of a liability than an asset. When the economy strengthens, and also when the dollar strengthens, the gold investor is in prime position to lose money.

When it comes to the science of investing in gold, the downside is contained. Gold won't always be the asset class that's outperforming—in fact, most of the time it's going to underperform—but it still serves its purpose as a hedge. When gold underperforms, the act of rebalancing forces you to buy into weakness. When it outperforms, the act of rebalancing forces you to sell into strength. When this strategy is maintained through multiple market cycles, there really is no downside to gold. It serves its purpose.

Everything changes when we move from science to art. In order for the rewards to get bigger, the game must become harder. Some investors are going to succeed at the art of investing in gold. Others are going to fail. In any one particular year, it's possible for the reward of investing in gold to be huge. Over time, we anticipate that other asset classes are going to perform better. That's why it's either used by the scientist as a hedge or by the artist as a speculative instrument.

The purpose of this chapter isn't to discredit everything we've learned. There are specific points in the economic cycle when gold outperforms. When this happens, it pays to be on the receiving side of the wealth transfer. It's easy to gloss over the notion of "specific points" and focus purely on the "wealth transfer." Doing so will get you in trouble. There have been and will continue to be extended periods when gold not only underperforms, but loses value not just in dollar terms, but also when measured against the Dow, the real estate market, and maybe even cryptocurrencies. If it didn't, we'd be completely hosed, because gold by nature is a hedge against economic catastrophe. We want gold to spend more time in bear territory than it spends in bull territory. Not just for the sake of our other investments, but for the sake of the economy, our jobs, our retirement plans, our social assistance programs, and everything else that has been baked into our economic infrastructure. To a large extent, both the scientist and the artist should be cheering against gold . . . *except for those specific points in the cycle when it pays to cheer for gold.*

If we want to really hone in on the downside of gold, we need to further ask ourselves, is gold the best hedge we have against inflation? Most of the time, the answer is no. During specific points, the answer is yes.

The dividend aristocrats are also a hedge against inflation. As the name implies, companies that belong to the dividend aristocrats pay a distribution. There's a compounding effect that increases over time, not solely through the act of reinvesting dividends, but also because these companies increase their dividend distribution annually. To be named a dividend aristocrat, the company must have a history of increasing their dividend payout each year for at least the past 25 years. This is great for investors. Not only does the dividend income increase over time, but the increase also puts upward pressure on the stock price, which can result in large capital gains. A long history of increasing the dividend is desirable because it can't be manipulated. There's no accounting trickery involved; the company has to actually come up with the cash to pay the dividend. If they've done this for 25-plus years, it's a sign of strength. We often say that past performance isn't a guarantee of future performance, but there are exceptions when this analogy simply isn't true.

A company that keeps increasing its dividend is more likely to continue on this path than a company that has never paid a dividend, but investors still need to remember that dividends can be cut at any time. There's no requirement for a company to keep paying a dividend on their common stock. Instead, we rely on these companies to maintain their coveted dividend aristocrat status, not just because it's good for the shareholder, but because it's good for the stock, which is ultimately good for the company.

The downside of investing in individual stocks, as opposed to precious metals, is that each stock must be evaluated separately. Companies can be mismanaged and the investor needs to acquire certain skills that will enable them to select a "winning" stock. With the right assortment of dividend aristocrats, it's possible to both hedge against inflation and benefit from the compounding effect of dividend income. It's only during those specific periods when fear simultaneously drives gold higher and stocks lower that we're better off investing in a non-income producing asset.

A similar observation can be made with bonds. As mentioned in Chapter 7, bonds are a better long-term hedge against inflation because the interest payments compound. It's during periods of hyperinflation that gold outperforms. While the return on U.S. Treasury bonds is typically lower than that of riskier issues, Treasuries are backed by the taxing authority of the United States. You'll never get this kind of backing with gold.

By now you're probably noticing a pattern. The downside to investing in gold doesn't pertain to gold alone, but to how gold behaves relative to other asset classes. There's an opportunity cost to holding gold. You miss out on the income that other assets generate, which means that it's only beneficial to pursue the art of investing in gold when the appreciation is expected to exceed both the appreciation and income that other assets provide.

Let's compare gold to real estate. A rental property is going to generate income and after the income is generated, you still have the rental property. There's no income with gold, but at the end of the day you still have the gold. Real estate has an obvious advantage, but the argument doesn't end there. With gold you never have to worry about clogged toilets in the middle of the night, unruly tenants who could trash the place and then sue you, insurance policies that have a clause against almost every type of natural disaster, or the horror of finding an overabundance of black mold in the basement. Gold is a headache-free investment. It never blindsides you with a surprise maintenance expense. The roof will never need replaced. The only question you need to ponder is, am I buying at a lower price than I'll eventually sell it for?

The real estate investor isn't so much looking to time the market (though they're not bashful about picking up a property on the cheap when the opportunity presents itself), but is instead looking to find a property that will generate income that exceeds both the mortgage and cost of maintenance. They're playing a different game than the gold investor. This game has the propensity to be much more challenging than the art of investing in gold because there are more variables. But if you do the work and master the art of finding the right property, employing the right property management company, and are able to earn positive cash flow, your existing properties will mostly run on autopilot. The new challenge is being able to do it again and again and again.

There are more numbers to crunch when it comes to real estate investing. When the numbers work in your favor, crunching them can be a lot of fun. It's best to crunch them on an after-tax basis because the U.S. tax code favors real estate, which makes sense, because real estate investors don't just act in their own self-interest, but also provide a service to a population of renters. The U.S. tax code essentially compensates them for taking care of all those clogged toilets by allowing them to depreciate the cost of the building. Land isn't depreciable, but the building is, and being able to take an annual tax deduction for the cost of this structure is a huge incentive for the real estate investor. The gold investor, as we'll see in Chapter 13, takes a beating on Tax Day.

It's not uncommon to earn double digit returns on rental real estate. This is a lucrative market. The long-term stock investor also does well. They should expect to earn average returns of roughly 10% per year, assuming they are exposed to the entire market. The long-term gold investor can't compete with these numbers. Over the past fifty years—which includes both the abolishment of the gold standard and the 26-year dry spell—the average annual return on gold comes in at 7.3%. With gold, the odds are stacked against you from the start. It's not just due to average returns, but the duration of time over which positive returns are earned. The stock market has longer bull runs than gold. It's easier to identify a stock market bull in its infancy and then ride it for a prolonged period of time. But when it's time for gold to outperform, it outperforms by a lot. In a short amount of time it can make rental payments look small. It can make dividends seem insignificant. It can make you wonder why you even considered speculating in cryptocurrencies. *And bonds?* Please. Even the double-digit yields that bond investors received in the 1980s are table scraps compared to what gold can do when fear and inflation are high. In the right environment, the gold investor doesn't merely outperform, but has wealth transferred to him. The game isn't going to last forever. Gold is a sprinter, which means it's going to run out of steam. When it does, it could be a while before it goes for its next run.

26-Year Dry Spell

If we really want to focus on the downside of gold, then we have no choice but to focus on the 26-year dry spell. We can't just prepare for the good times (which in this case, equates to bad times for other investments, not to mention the economy, the job market, and our currency). We can't spend our entire investment careers anticipating that wealth will eventually be transferred to those invested in gold. During that same 26-year period, retirements could have been built on the momentum of other assets classes.

Put another way, from 1980 through 2006, gold suffered through a 26-year period when the tactics discussed in this book simply wouldn't work. Those who subscribed to the science of investing in gold did fine. They sold other asset classes into strength as they bought into the weakness of gold. Even though it took 26 years to recover, the volatility that gold exhibited while nestled in the doldrums still served a benefit to the asset allocator. It facilitated the act of trading back and forth between asset classes. A small rise in gold enables the asset allocator to sell into a moderate level of strength, as the following dip enables them to trade back into subdued weakness. The asset allocator still benefits from short spurts of volatility. There's a greater benefit when markets are given time to work through their prolonged secular cycles, but smaller gyrations also provide a benefit.

The scientist perseveres while the artist could potentially starve. That's the downside of being an artist. The tactics discussed in this book enable them to exploit hiccups in the economic cycle. They enable them to take side bets and increase their holdings when gold is *likely* to outperform. There can be years, even decades, when the tactics we've discussed should not be implemented. Knowledge of gold and how the market functions is just a portion of the successful investor's acumen. It's not the only way to build wealth and at times, it's counterproductive to try. The asset allocator will survive. If you're trading the Dow/gold ratio, remember to increase your exposure to gold as the ratio rises above 15 and decrease your exposure as the ratio falls back towards 5. Once your exposure is reduced, years could pass before it's time to buy more gold.

Don't get discouraged when the strategies we've discussed aren't applicable. There's no sense in arguing with the market. It's always right. We're either right along with it or we're wrong in opposition to it. When the market indicators discussed in Chapter 7 aren't chiming, it means that it's time to do something else. Hold an income producing asset. Or hold cash. While we know that a fiat currency is going to lose value over time, it's still better to hold cash than to hold an asset that's working against you. When you can't find an attractive investment, cash is the place to be.

The downside of *REALLY* needing the protection that gold provides

Maybe your goal isn't to exploit the short spurts of time during which gold outperforms. Perhaps your financial concerns are few in number and what you really want from gold is protection in case a catastrophe ruins your otherwise rosy situation. You're not trying to build wealth, but instead taking measures to protect what you already have. The only thing you want from gold is protection from a collapse of the financial system. You could care less if gold is up or down at any specific point in time. In line with Warren Buffett's observation, you're content with your gold just sitting there looking pretty. It's even better if no one knows you have it. So you join the prophets of doom and gloom. You take physical possession of your gold and you bury it in your back yard.

Now, let's say those bad times actually arrive. I'm not talking about a measly little recession or even a deep depression. What I'm talking about is financial Armageddon, something significantly worse than the Great Depression. Fiat currencies have failed. Banks have closed their doors. All ETFs have been rendered worthless (including the gold ETFs). The cryptocurrency market imploded eons ago, just like the market for tulips. This is why we take physical possession of our bullion. It's the reserve currency. When paper money is rendered worthless, it's the only form of currency left. But here's the thing, we're in a depression that's so deep that no one wants gold. We're all fighting for basic human necessities like food, shelter, and clothing. These are the only items that hold value. Gold just sits there and looks pretty.

During the Great Depression, the U.S. dollar was on the gold standard. Gold was money. It wasn't an investment that people turn to for exponential returns during periods when the value of our currency deteriorates. Since switching over to a fiat currency, we have yet to struggle through anything that's even remotely comparable to the Great Depression, yet the prophets of doom and gloom still exist. They do more than just hedge with gold. They do more than try to build wealth at specific intervals when other assets fail to perform. Instead, they cling to gold as though it will provide protection when everything else fails. It's not just individuals, but central banks too. The International Monetary Fund is in the same camp. *But will gold prove to be a safe haven should EVERYTHING else fail?*

My prediction is that gold will continue to provide exponential returns during economic downturns as long as we maintain the ability to contain the downturn. For this reason, gold is a winning investment at certain stages of the economic cycle. Should the downturn become worse than anything we've experienced in our lifetime, it's possible that no one will give you anything for the gold that you hold for protection. We could conceivably enter territory where fiat currency is considered safer, should people continue to subscribe to the ideology that they can trade dollars for food, shelter, and clothing.

Never put all of your eggs in one basket. When economic indicators suggest that it's time to overweight in favor of gold, go ahead and do so, but do so with an understanding of the risk involved. Never risk more than you can afford to lose. And never go all-in on a single asset class. When the odds are clearly stacked in your favor, diversification will save you from the fallacy of being wrong about those odds.

We place value on gold because the supply is believed to be fixed. There's only so much above the earth and there's only so much below the earth. What about gold on other planets? The next gold rush likely won't be in California. We know that gold exists on meteorites. What about Mars? On Mercury? Or even Venus? This might sound like the premise of a science fiction movie, but given the rate of technological advancements, we could be exploring previously uncharted solar territory sooner than we anticipate. If they strike gold, they strike gold. Given what we know about the emotion of human greed, should gold be found, they'll find a way to bring it back to earth. It might not happen within the next few decades, but there's also no guarantee that it won't.

Chapter 12: What To Do After You've Built Wealth With Gold

Building wealth with gold is very achievable. If you follow the economy and pay attention to economic indicators, then your ability to build wealth with this asset class is mostly dependent on when the opportunity arrives. It can't be forced. At some point in time, the economic indicators will flash. Fear will be evident and inflation will be coming. When gold gets dragged down because of a stock market crash, chances are good that gold will rebound quickly. When gold takes off ahead of the gold miners, chances are good that the gold mining stocks are going to rally even harder. These are great opportunities, but they can't be forced. When it's there, it's there.

Eventually, wealth will be built, which begs the obvious question, *now what?* We know that the prophets of doom and gloom will encourage you bury some gold in your back yard. If you've built significant wealth, placing some of your earnings in bullion, be it with a vaulting service or a strategically concealed safe inside your home, isn't a bad idea. It might not produce any income, but it will be there when you need it.

In *Beating The Market*, I discuss making changes to your investment strategy as your portfolio gets bigger. The strategy used to build wealth should be different from the strategy used to protect wealth. In this case, we invested our discretionary income in gold when we were confident that it would pay off. Now that it's paid off, let's do something with the money that isn't as risky as trying to time the gold market. Gold can still be used as a portfolio hedge, but aside from that, we now have more to lose than to gain.

Once you reach the point where the income on your investments covers your living expenses, your tolerance for risk should be drastically reduced. It never hurts to set up a separate brokerage account to take some high-risk positions with your play money, but for the most part, once you've built sufficient wealth, your focus should be on protecting that wealth. Invest in stable blue-chip companies that pay dividends. Buy Treasury bonds that are backed by the taxing authority of the U.S. government. Acquire a rental property in a nice neighborhood. Hedge these investments with a modest allocation to gold. Then, when fear sets in and high inflation is imminent, increasing your exposure to gold is completely optional. Chances are, the stable blue-chip companies will continue to pay dividends, even if stock prices take a temporary dip. Treasury bonds are still going to pay what they're supposed to pay, even if the economic outlook is dreary. And your tenants still need a place to live, even if the housing market isn't on the up-and-up. You used to view economic downturns as an opportunity that enabled you to build wealth. Now that you've used the returns on your gold investments to build a portfolio of income-producing assets, you're wondering if the risk is still worth it. If I've done my job adequately, you have the appropriate tools at your disposal to make this decision.

This chapter is short for a reason. It's not because the options of how you might invest your earnings are few, but because they're beyond the scope of this book. It's difficult to specialize strictly in gold because the opportunities to earn large returns from gold are limited in frequency. It's because of these once-in-a-decade opportunities that being knowledgeable of gold holds value. When gold isn't paying off, we need to be knowledgeable of other asset classes. After gold has paid off, preservation of capital should be the cornerstone of your investment strategy.

For most, investing in gold isn't a life-long pursuit, but a means to an end when all the pieces fall into place. You have to seize the day when it's ripe to be seized. From there, it pays to specialize in something that can actually serve as a life-long investment. Stocks and real estate are notable options. They have the propensity to provide consistent cash flow, even when markets are volatile. They enable the investor to remove market timing from the equation in order to focus on other life pursuits.

Chapter 13: Taxes

Like the previous chapter, I'm going to keep this as brief as possible, but for a very different reason. It's not that taxation on gold is overly complicated and beyond the scope of this book. It's actually quite simple. That's the first reason this will be brief. The second, of course, is that taxes are boring. Raise your hand if you'd have read this book if it was titled *The Art and Science of Paying Taxes on Gold.* I'm confident that no one accidently dropped their book or device just now. Nonetheless, we're going to discuss taxes, and when we're finished you'll be in a better position to earn the largest possible after-tax return.

When you think about it, this could have been part of the previous chapter. If you're really wondering what people do after they build wealth with gold, the answer is they pay taxes. Not only that, they pay more taxes than their friends are paying on stocks and real estate—*all the more reason to specialize in a different area once the wealth has been built.*

In the U.S., precious metals are considered collectibles, just like art, rare books, baseball cards, and fine wine. Provided you hold the collectible for at least a year, the capital gains tax will be 28%. If you ask me, this is ludicrous. Aside from the coin collector, we invest in gold for the same reason that we invest in stocks. It's not a collection, it's an addition to a portfolio of securities. Long-term capital gains should therefore be taxed at no more than 20%, like with stocks. This is a reasonable argument, but it won't get you anywhere. Uncle Sam is going to slap you with a 28% tax when you sell gold for a gain. Think of it as a punishment for losing faith in the U.S. dollar. What truly sends the price of gold higher is when the central banks buy in large quantities. This action increases taxes that are collected from individual investors, but the central banks aren't taxed on their gains.

Getting around this punishment tax isn't difficult. Holding an ETF like the GLD in an IRA, 401(k), or other tax-preferred account can provide significant tax savings. Physical bullion can also be purchased in a tax-preferred account, as can rare books, expensive art, and fine wine.

Another way around the punishment tax is to invest in gold mining stocks. By doing so, you're not acquiring a "collectible" but instead, investing in companies that mine the collectible. It's an equity interest. The gold miners are running a business and you're acquiring an ownership interest in this business. As a result, your gains will be taxed the same as with any other stock investment. If you invest in both gold and gold mining stocks, the gold should be held in a tax-preferred account and the gold mining stocks should be held in a regular taxable account.

Gold is a physical asset. This comes with both advantages and disadvantages. While I wholeheartedly believe that a broadly diversified position in the stock market should be the nucleus of an investment portfolio, I also believe that all investors should hold at least some physical assets. Should we all wake up one day to find that our online brokerage accounts have been scrubbed from the Internet, we still have something that we can put our hands on. It's comforting. When it comes to physical assets, most investors turn to either gold or real estate. Gold, of course, can be purchased in much smaller increments. It's easier to gradually increase exposure over time. But when it comes to taxes, real estate is the champion. We discussed the benefits in the previous chapter. Not only does the real estate investor avoid being taxed at 28%, they also get to depreciate the cost of their buildings over 27 ½ years. Just think about the difference. The gold investor can hold gold for as long as they want without paying any tax, but when they sell, the gain is taxed at 28%. The real estate investor also defers the gain on their property until the point of sale, but gets to deduct depreciation while they wait. At the point of sale, the real estate investor is taxed at no more than 20% on the gain. It can be argued that the real estate investor pays tax on their rental income along the way. This is true, but the fact that they earned rental income is another advantage in favor of real estate.

Uncle Sam doesn't want you to invest in gold. He wants you to invest in real estate. Given that rental real estate is an income producing asset that receives tax advantages, it's difficult for gold to keep up, except for those intervals in the economic cycle when just about everything except gold takes a hit. When that happens, you're comparing massive returns on gold to modest income on real estate.

The fact that gold can serve as a modest hedge or be used to time specific intervals of the economic cycle isn't just supported by how gold behaves relative to other asset classes, but is also supported by the tax code. That's the art and science of investing in gold. Uncle Sam gets it and he's going to tax you accordingly.

A Final Note to the Reader

Still have questions? That's fine. Investing can pose many challenges. There is no single book that will answer all of your questions. Like anything in life, success with your investments is a process of continual learning followed by proper implementation. Don't just read one book about investing. Do what I do and read as many of them as you can.

We have plenty of resources available at www.theselfmadeinvestor.com. We offer tools to help you benchmark and rebalance your portfolio. We publish book recommendations for further reading. The books we recommend are the same books that I've learned from myself, and we only review books that will provide value to our readers. The blog posts, of course, are free. So there's no reason why a fee-conscious investor wouldn't want to pay us a visit.

You can also follow us on Twitter at https://twitter.com/MadeInvestor. If you still have questions, please feel free to shoot me an email: theselfmadeinvestor@gmail.com

As a self-published author, I rely on reviews to sell my work. If you feel that the material presented in *The Art and Science of Investing in Gold* will provide value to other readers, please leave a review on Amazon. Your support is greatly appreciated!

Made in the USA
Monee, IL
06 November 2026

68010590R00121